the
kimchi

chronicles

the kimchi

chronicles

Korean Cooking for an American Kitchen

Marja Vongerichten

with Julia Turshen

PRINCIPAL PHOTOGRAPHY BY Andre Baranowski
FOREWORD BY Jean-Georges Vongerichten

RODALE

© 2011 by Marja Vongerichten and Frappé Inc.
Principal photography © 2011 by Andre Baranowski

Additional photographs by Tom Caltabiano, Pil Oh, and Seyoung Oh—see page 238 for full credits

Rodale books may be purchased for business or promotional use or for special sales. For information, please write to: Special Markets Department, Rodale, Inc., 733 Third Avenue, New York, NY 10017

Printed in the United States of America
Rodale Inc. makes every effort to use acid-free ⊗, recycled paper ♻.

Book design by Kara Plikaitis

Library of Congress Cataloging-in-Publication Data

Vongerichten, Marja.
  The kimchi chronicles : Korean cooking for an American kitchen / Marja Vongerichten ; foreword by Jean-Georges Vongerichten.
    p.   cm.
  Includes index.
  ISBN 978-1-60961-127-9 hardcover
  1. Cooking, Korean—United States.   2. Cookbooks.   I. Title.
TX724.5.K65V66 2011
641.59519—dc22   2011010865

Distributed to the trade by Macmillan

2 4 6 8 10 9 7 5 3   hardcover

We inspire and enable people to improve their lives and the world around them.
www.rodalebooks.com

This book is dedicated to my two mothers,
one who gave me life and the other who helped me live it.

Contents

Foreword

When I was growing up in Alsace, France, my room was just above the kitchen. My mother and grandmother used to prepare meals for the family's coal company employees. Big pots of traditional Alsatian foods bubbled below, and the scent would just waft up into my room. I loved watching them cook, and eventually I became the family palate—I'd taste the food and tell my mom what was missing: a little salt here, a little butter there. One day, I realized that I wanted to cook for a living, and I was lucky enough to apprentice with some of the greatest chefs in France. I was trained in classical French techniques, which were firmly based in stocks that took hours to make and were heavy on the butter and cream.

When I was 23, I moved to Bangkok to work at the Mandarin Oriental. It was the first time that I had ever traveled that far from home. On my way to the hotel from the airport, I stopped at a food stand on the side of the street and had a simple soup that changed my life. This woman put a pot over a portable burner, added some water, lemongrass, a little shrimp, and in minutes whipped up one of the most flavorful broths I had ever tasted. It went against everything I had learned, and from that moment all I wanted to do was to go into the markets to explore these new flavors. Endless chiles and spices, new fruits and vegetables that I had never seen before, it was all there for me to discover. It transformed the way that I cooked, and today I continue to be inspired by these bright and intense flavors.

When I met Marja, my life changed in every way, even expanding my palate. Falling in love with her meant falling in love with Korean food, even though it took me some time to come around. When we moved in together, I opened the refrigerator and was turned off by a completely overpowering aroma. (Anyone who's had a jar of kimchi in their fridge knows what I'm talking about.) I gave it a taste, though, and now I'm addicted. It reminds me of the sauerkraut of my childhood, but even better because it's got a spicy kick. Actually, the more Korean food I eat, the more I realize how similar it is to Alsatian food. Both rely heavily on cabbage and pork; both emphasize frugality and seasonality; both are unpretentious and satisfying. I've even started playing with dishes that combine the two cuisines, including a Korean version of Alsatian *baeckeoffe* (page 127).

Traveling to Korea with Marja to tape *Kimchi Chronicles* allowed me to discover the origins of many of the meals I love that Marja makes at home, like *bulgogi* and chicken braised with vegetables and *gochujang*, the red pepper paste that's the backbone of the Korean kitchen. Like the food I tried in Thailand years ago, Korean cooking allows you to achieve deep, developed flavors in a relatively short time, which, incidentally, makes it great for entertaining. On weekends in our country home, the kitchen counter is filled with simple, comforting Korean dishes that our friends and family devour. Marja often makes *bindaetteok* (page 67) to eat with cocktails, which lately consist of freshly squeezed grapefruit juice mixed with Korean *soju*. Sometimes I'll grill something simple, like a good steak, and we'll eat it with whatever vegetables are in season and some rice and kimchi on the side.

I've incorporated Korean food not just into my personal life, but also into my professional repertoire. I'm working on putting a hot dog with kimchi relish like the one on page 86 on the menu at the Mercer Kitchen—it's the perfect balance of sweet and sour, a relish that takes the dog to a whole new level. My son Cedric, who is the executive chef at Perry Street, now serves a dish with a sauce made of butter and *gochujang*. At Spice Market, my Fast, Hot Kimchi (page 42) comes tucked underneath a nicely seared piece of fish, giving it just the right spicy bite.

Korean food is Marja's passion, and it has been one of the most important ways for her to reconnect with her roots. I've followed her through her journey, and have been lucky to learn about the flavors and traditions of Korean cuisine. Today, we're excited to be able to share all that we've learned and have come to love about Korean foods and traditions not only with the *Kimchi Chronicles* television show, but also with this cookbook. We both hope that you'll enjoy the journey as much as we have.

Jean-Georges Vongerichten, winter 2011

"Everyone has a right to know his roots—from whence he came.

It helps us formulate a concept of who we are and determine where we want to go."

—Margo McKay

Introduction

How did I, little old me from Uijeongbu, Korea, end up hosting a public television series on Korean food and culture and writing a Korean cookbook? It starts, as many good things do, in a restaurant—in this instance a place on Manhattan's Columbus Circle called Jean-Georges owned by my husband, Jean-Georges Vongerichten. I was talking with Charlie Pinsky and Eric Rhee, friends of JG's who produced the wonderful public television series *Spain . . . On the Road Again* among many others. They were looking for a new project to follow up on the success of that one, and had in mind a series about Korea, a country they considered long overdue for wider exposure and rife with intriguing food, culture, and sites. They knew that I had been born in Korea to a Korean mother, was adopted and raised in the States, and have spent my adult life reuniting with my Korean family, often using food as a means to understanding my background and my culture. When they offered me the opportunity to introduce the ingredients, customs, and people of my native country to a larger audience, I said *all right*!

During the last year I've traveled all over Korea with a terrific crew and also brought them into my home kitchen in New York to re-create some of the flavors and dishes we had encountered overseas for my public television series, *Kimchi Chronicles*. We've even invited some fun companions along for the journey, including our neighbors Hugh and Deb Jackman and my sweet friend Heather Graham. At the end of it all I'm thrilled to have created so many converts to the pleasures of the Korean table, and to show those not familiar with the foods and logistics of a Korean meal how well this style of eating fits with the way many of us like to eat today.

I am passionate about Korean cuisine's approachability and health benefits, about the way everyone eats together and shares everything, about the way it has connected me so closely with so many people in my life.

In a sense you might say that I myself am a somewhat recent convert to the joys of Korean food, having been raised on the typical American diet for most of my first two decades. The earliest record of my existence is a birth certificate dated August 7, 1979 (although I was born on March 15, 1976). My mother Yong Ye

Me, at 1½ months old with my
birth mother and at the orphanage

was a 19-year-old Korean woman, my father an African-American serviceman who abandoned her when she was 7 months pregnant with me. Left alone with an infant and no financial support, she faced incredible hardship.

But I was one of the lucky ones. After spending the first 3 years of my life with my mother, I was adopted by loving American parents. My father, Colonel James Phillip Allen Jr. (who was newly married to my mother Margo McKay), was a United States marine stationed in Korea. At the time of my adoption there were many reports of struggling Amerasians, kids who, like me, were the offspring of the numerous and, too often, careless American military officers who were serving there. Reports of the desperate difficulty of our situation led my parents to the St. Vincent's Home for Amerasians, an orphanage where my birth mother had brought me when she realized she wouldn't be able to give me the life she felt I deserved. For a mixed-race child born to a mother without formal education, the climate at the time was by no means accepting or supportive.

Me, at 3½, at home in Korea in a traditional hanbok and with my parents, James Allen and Margo McKay

My first meal with my adoptive parents was at a US army base. I had a hot dog (I ate just the bun and left the meat), a Coke, and vanilla ice cream. One month later I officially had a legal name, Marja (a combination of the names Margo and James), and left my original name, Brenda Bae, behind. After living in Korea for almost a year, I eventually left my birth country behind and moved to suburban northern Virginia.

Fast-forward 17 years. I had always wanted to know my birth mother, but it wasn't until I was in college that I was willing to take the practical steps to find her. I was feeling independent and ready to go on what would turn out to be an extraordinary journey. Fortunately my parents had kept meticulous records of my adoption, a sign of extraordinary respect and compassion both for me and for my birth mother that made it possible for us to reconnect so many years later.

Through the Korean embassy in Washington DC, I was ultimately able to track down my mother's telephone number, which to my amazement turned out to be an American number with a Brooklyn area code! It took me 3 hours to work up the nerve to call her for the first time and about another month to venture to New York to see her.

Our first reunion in New York was, needless to say, an emotional experience. Seeing each other for the first time in so many years, so many years during which I had grown up without her, was both shocking and comfortable. It felt as though I were coming home, even though we were thousands of miles away from Korea. We went to her apartment in Brooklyn and she made *bulgogi*, a popular Korean dish of marinated thinly sliced beef that she served with *chonggak kimchi,* a kimchi made with Korean ponytail radishes. Although I hadn't eaten authentic Korean food in almost 2 decades, the meal was strangely familiar; the food I had eaten for the first 3 years of my life had taken root in my subconscious, and reawakening those sensory memories helped me feel connected to my mother.

My rediscovery of Korean food actually began several years earlier, when I was about 14. I was grocery shopping for my family at our local supermarket in Virginia, one of my favorite weekly chores, when I spotted a jar of kimchi. I snuck it into the shopping cart, eager for some kind of connection to the place where I was born and raised, but also worried that being excited about Korean food would feel like a betrayal to my parents. As soon as I got home I surreptitiously opened the jar and took a bite. The flavor—pungent, fiery, sour, earthy, full of garlic— seemed to speak directly to a part of me that I felt, but couldn't quite articulate. I had a similar response to a Chinese takeout dish of noodles with black bean sauce that my father often ordered. The flavors of garlic and ginger, of chile and soy sauce were not distinctly Korean like kimchi, yet when I ate this dish, my taste buds began talking to me. I later found out from my birth mother that *jajangmyeon* (a Korean-Chinese hybrid dish of chewy noodles with black bean sauce) had been one of my favorite things to eat as a young child. In fact I loved it so much that she bought it for me twice a week, no small expense for her. To this day, it's still one of my most favorite comfort foods.

I started cooking Korean food myself after moving to New York when I was 20. Every Sunday my birth mother and I would go to K-Town in Manhattan to

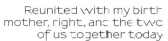

Reunited with my birth
mother, right, and the two
of us together today

stock up on Korean ingredients and she would cook all sorts of Korean dishes during the week. I also traveled to Korea several times, trips that consisted almost entirely of eating with my biological family (with breaks for karaoke!), all of whom were eager to share their memories of what I ate as a baby in Korea.

Food was and continues to be a bridge between my Korean identity and my life in America, especially when I eat and cook with my mother and my extended Korean family, and when I introduce my American family to Korean food. At home in New York, I've continued to cook Korean food with increasing frequency, even converting Jean-Georges and our daughter, Chloe, to the wonders of kimchi and *gochujang* (red pepper paste).

For me, life has come full circle and I have more love in this world than I could ever have hoped for. Sharing meals with my family in Korea, cooking and eating with my Korean birth mother in New York, and introducing all of the dishes and rituals to my American family and extended French family have taught me

My daughter, Chloe, and Chloe
with Jean-Georges at his
namesake restaurant

that our different cultures are more intertwined than we can possibly imagine. These meals demonstrate over and over again the importance of food and how it brings us together and helps us to define who we are. No matter where we're from, we all value sitting at the table together, eating dishes that we grew up with, dishes that we've spontaneously created by combining ingredients from our multicultural pantry. We love to see the similarities in seemingly incongruous cultures— Koreans and Alsatians like my husband both use cabbage and pork in just about everything! The kitchen, in other words, is the perfect arena to celebrate cultural richness.

My hope is that you will come to know the joys of Korean cuisine, the fiery, fermented, strong flavors, as well as the more subtle dishes, the easy soups and simple grilled meats, the elegant noodles, and the brilliant hangover cures. I have re-created all of these Korean recipes in my American kitchen with an American sensibility. And my husband, who knows a thing or two when it comes to cooking,

has put a Korean spin on many of his standbys—including tuna tartare (page 149) and even an Alsatian dish called *baeckeoffe* (page 127)—showing both the subtlety and the versatility of seemingly exotic flavor agents like *gochujang* and *gochugaru*. You can make all of these recipes with ingredients that are probably already on your grocery list (for the small handful that might not be, check out "Pantry: My Korean-American Kitchen" on page 1.

Don't feel you have to jump in the deep end if you are new to Korean cooking. Incorporate one or two Korean dishes into your regular menus (like a big bowl of spicy *kimchi jjigae* stew (page 58) or thin and crispy Seafood and Scallion Pajeon pancakes (page 151) . . . or serve up a selection of your own favorite salads in a Korean-inspired *banchan* spread. Try one of the barbecue recipes in Chapter Three for your next summer cookout and invite friends in for a warming bowl of noodles after a late evening out or a cold winter hike Get to know the ingredients and use them to add excitement and variety to your own go-to recipes. Cook and season according to your own preferences Korean cuisine is not based on precision, so be daring and experiment.

The Kimchi Chronicles has been a delicious journey of rediscovery for me, and one I hope you will want to take yourself, with me as your guide.

Gunbae!

—Marja Vongerichten

Author's Note on Translations

Translation, like cooking, is often more of an art than a science. Therefore, it's important to note that translating Korean words and phrases to written English is a subjective thing, as there are no official, established conventions. I've aimed to include Korean names and terms wherever possible, but please note that the spellings I've chosen are not the only ones you'll find—it's like spelling to taste.

for Kids

Korean food, with all of its spice and pickles and fermented and dried foods, might seem off-putting to children, but I've found it to be a surprisingly kid-friendly world of food. My daughter, Chloe, a notoriously picky eater, counts rice wrapped in Korean seaweed as one of her favorite snacks and she even loves kimchi. As with most foods, it's helpful to introduce a variety of flavors and textures to kids starting at a young age in small doses. (I've even heard of mothers dipping kimchi into water to make it less pungent, almost the way French mothers serve youngsters wine diluted with lots of water.) *Mandu*, or Korean dumplings, are also really popular with kids, and all of the Korean barbecue is a hit (put anything on a skewer and kids seem to go crazy, especially if you let them cook their own dinner!). Eating *banchan*, the array of small cold salads and vegetable dishes that precede almost every Korean meal, is a great way to introduce your children to all sorts of things—the small plates encourage small tastes. It's not as overwhelming as a big plate of something new and unusual.

Pantry:
My Korean-American Kitchen

My home kitchen is a literal melting pot, a place of multicultural eating that keeps my family connected to our Korean, French, and American roots. This rich diversity is reflected in the contents of my pantry, and the ingredients we consider staples. My husband keeps great olive oil and European vinegars in the cupboard for dressing salads; chocolate hidden among the condiments as a bedtime snack (he can't go to sleep without having a little bit); and buttermilk in the fridge for pancakes on the weekends. I keep kimchi in the refrigerator, and while everyone gave me a hard time at first, it's become a household staple; even our daughter, Chloe, whose ideal meal would probably be pasta with a side of white rice, loves kimchi. I also keep fish sauce next to the vinegar, dried anchovies tucked on a shelf next to the rice, and pounds (literally) of *gochugaru* (red pepper powder) that I haul back from Korea in my suitcase. Our cheese drawer probably says the most about our family—there's Parmigiano-Reggiano for Chloe's spaghetti, immaculate goat cheeses that Jean-Georges brings home from his restaurants, and individually wrapped American cheese slices, which are my Korean family's secret ingredient in many traditional Korean soups (see page 61 for more on that).

One of the most appealing aspects of Korean food is its accessibility. Even though it may seem incredibly exotic, requiring lots of unfamiliar ingredients and preparations, at its core it's a flavorful, healthy, approachable cuisine that you can make using many of the ingredients you already have in your pantry. As a matter of fact, there are really only two essential ingredients I find myself using over and over again that might not already be in your kitchen—*gochujang* (red pepper paste) and *gochugaru* (red pepper powder). The good news is both are easy to get online and are on the shelves of every Korean grocery store and lots of specialty grocery stores. Since both keep indefinitely you can stock up whenever you find a good source so you'll never have to scramble at the last minute.

In the following pages, you'll find descriptions of the ingredients used in Korean cooking that might be unfamiliar. I've also given a list of my must-have cooking tools (including scissors!) and a list of resources.

Pantry Staples

Gochujang (Red Pepper Paste)

This fermented hot pepper paste is the most indispensable, distinctly Korean, and frequently used ingredient in the Korean cook's pantry. It's made primarily of *gochugaru* (red pepper powder) bound with sweet rice powder (which lends a bit of sweetness) and seasoned with salt. After it's been left to ferment, the flavor and red color become dark and rich. Labor-intensive to make, *gochujang* is almost always bought packaged rather than prepared at home (sort of like Americans and ketchup). It's used in just about every sauce, marinade, soup, and braise; it goes on poultry, beef, pork, seafood, tofu, and more. In other words, it's the MVP in every Korean kitchen and on every Korean table.

Gochugaru (Red Pepper Powder)

Although *gochugaru* is now ubiquitous in Korean cooking, it wasn't widely available in Korea until the 1600s. The red chile we've come to associate so strongly with Korean food came originally from Latin America, traveling to Asia through Spanish commerce. I think the best *gochugaru* comes from the area around Sokcho, where my most of my biological family lives. It comes coarsely ground or finely ground; I always use coarse in my cooking, but you can substitute fine if you'd like. *Gochugaru* is worth seeking out for your Korean cooking at home since it's much fruitier and milder than most commercially available chile powders (which is why I'm often generous with how much I use). In a pinch, you can substitute red pepper flakes (like those offered to shake on pizza), but use them to taste, as they're much spicier than *gochugaru*.

Doenjang (Soybean Paste)

Made of fermented soybeans, *doenjang*, which translates to "thick paste," is essentially Korean miso paste. It's distinguished from Japanese miso by its coarse, unrefined texture and its aggressive flavor—this isn't subtle stuff. It's often fermented outdoors in large stone pots. In Andong, we went to a restaurant, known for its homemade *doenjang*, that was run by Grandmother Chung, whose family has been making it for 19 generations! It was hard to miss—their driveway is filled with 3,000 clay pots of the stuff. You can substitute Japanese miso paste for *doenjang* with successful results (especially if you can find a coarse Japanese variety).

Ssamjang

A thick, slightly spicy paste, *ssamjang* is basically a mixture of *gochujang* and *doenjang*, but it can also

GOCHUGARU / SESAME SEEDS / SALT

GOCHUJANG

DOENJANG

With Grandmother Chung at her restaurant in Andong

be flavored with sesame oil, garlic, or, sometimes, brown sugar. It's used as a condiment for grilled meats and is essential for *bo ssam* (page 91).

Kimchi and Kimchi Liquid

While making kimchi at home is fun and completely doable (page 37), most Koreans buy prepared kimchi at markets and grocery stores. I keep both my own homemade kimchi and my favorite store-bought varieties in my refrigerator at all times. The liquid that covers the kimchi is a terrific seasoning on its own and I use it often in dishes like *bindaetteok* (page 67) and kimchi butter (page 81). Many of my recipes call for "sour kimchi," which essentially means old kimchi. Just like the distinction between a sour pickle and a half-sour pickle, older kimchi takes on a stronger, more acidic flavor that I find very welcome in dishes like *kimchi jjigae* (page 58). If you don't like the developed flavor of sour kimchi, feel free to substitute lighter tasting fresh kimchi.

Soy Sauce

Like most Asian cooks, Koreans use soy sauce (made from soybeans fermented with water and salt) as a key seasoning. A dash of soy sauce transforms any dish just the way salt does, but with an added backbone. This depth of flavor is referred to by the Japanese as umami. I often call for "high-quality" soy sauce in my recipes, by which I mean a reliable brand that doesn't list MSG as an ingredient.

Toasted Sesame Oil

Toasted sesame oil, derived from toasted and crushed sesame seeds, is distinguished by its nutty, rich flavor. It's often used as a seasoning rather than an oil for cooking, but I like to cook with it since all the dishes I make that start with it take on a great depth of flavor.

Fish Sauce

Made from fermented fish, fish sauce has a smell that can be off-putting to most first-timers, but its salty, funky, distinctive taste borders on addictive. It's got the same umami thing going on as soy sauce.

Vinegar

Acidity is nearly as important as salt in Korean (and most all) cooking. A splash of vinegar elevates flavors and perks everything up. Koreans often use mild apple vinegar, not to be confused with apple cider vinegar. Rice vinegar is equally common and

RICE VINEGAR

SOY SAUCE

TOASTED
SESAME OIL

APPLE
VINEGAR

F SH SAUCE

I use both in my kitchen; for the recipes in this book, however, I have called for rice vinegar as it's more readily available. Feel free to substitute apple vinegar if you do come across it.

Korean Hot Mustard

A vital condiment to be served with *naengmyeon* (page 200), a cold noodle soup with brisket, Korean hot mustard is very similar to hot French mustard as well as the Chinese version. If you can't find it, I find that powdered Colman's mustard mixed with water, vinegar, and salt makes an excellent substitute.

Roasted Sesame Seeds

Roasted sesame seeds are vital to Korean cooking, adding toasty flavor and crunchy texture in a variety of dishes. They're sometimes cooked into soups and stews, ground into marinades, and often sprinkled over dishes not merely for aesthetic purposes but also for a great taste. While I always buy them already roasted (they come in jars), you can purchase raw sesame seeds and toast them in a dry skillet or in the oven if you prefer.

Dashida (Jomiryo)

A granulated instant beef stock powder, *dashida* (also known as *jomiryo*) is often used as a seasoning, almost like salt with more depth. Since many commercial brands contain MSG, be careful about which you choose. If you do not eat meat but do eat fish, I find that an equal amount of fish sauce can stand in for *dashida* to add that salty, savory quality.

Dried Anchovy and Kelp Packets

Dried anchovies are used often in Korean cooking; in fact, small ones are often eaten whole as a snack. Large dried anchovies are the base for anchovy stock, which typically also includes dried seaweed. One of my favorite discoveries in the Korean supermarket I frequent in New Jersey was the packets of dried anchovies and kelp that I have come to think of as savory tea bags. You can pop a few into a pot of boiling water and have flavorful stock in no time. The best part is the packet makes it so easy—there's no need to measure the amounts and no need to strain the stock. Just fish the packet out and discard.

Seaweed

Seaweed, one of the healthiest foods you can consume because it's full of minerals, is used a lot in Korean cooking. *Gim* is dried laver seaweed that gets sprinkled on top of noodle soups and wrapped around rice to make *gimbap* (page 181). (Japanese nori, also a laver, is a widely used substitute.) Dried *miyeok* is my go-to for soups like Birthday Seaweed Soup (page 57), but you can substitute many types of dried seaweed, such as wakame, available in health food stores or Asian markets. Dried kelp—*dasima* in Korean or *kombu* in Japanese—is great for stocks.

MIYEOK SEAWEED

SALTED SHRIMP

GIM

Salted Shrimp

Known as *saeujeot* in Korean, salted shrimp are a common ingredient in kimchi and are also used in *bo ssam* (page 91), a grand dish of pork belly wrapped in lettuce with other seasonings. Unlike dried, salted shrimp used in other Asian cuisines, Korean salted shrimp come in a jar packed in liquid that you drain before using.

Salt

I use coarse, kosher salt in all of my cooking.

DAECHU

MARMALADE

Dried Dates (Daechu)

Also known as jujubes, these are dark red and wrinkled. They are often used medicinally (they're said to help relax you) as well as in many popular dishes like *samgyetang* (page 141) and Braised Short Ribs with Pumpkin (page 123). Dried cherries make a reasonable substitute.

Honey Citron Marmalade

Koreans often drink a delicious tea made of hot water combined with a jellylike ingredient called *yujacha,* which is a honey-sweetened marmalade made of citron. Not only does it make a great drink, it's also a terrific ingredient for dressings and marinades, such as the dipping sauce for Crunchy Fried Squid (page 168) and the Barbecued Chicken with Sweet Barbecue Sauce (page 94). A good-quality orange marmalade makes a perfect substitute.

Perilla Seeds

Perilla seeds come from the perilla plant, which is often labeled "sesame plant." It is a member of the mint family and is not at all related to the plant that bears sesame seeds. It's its own wonderful thing, and the seeds have a flavor reminiscent of sesame, but also with the tang of coriander seeds. Perilla seeds are a terrific ingredient to experiment with, but if you can't find them and want to make a recipe like the Pork Neck Stew with Potatoes and Perilla (page 135), you can substitute a combination of sesame and coriander seeds.

 SOJU

 SOJU

 MAKGEOLLI

 MAKGEOLLI

Soju

One of the most popular alcoholic beverages in Korea, *soju* has a flavor similar to vodka but is a bit sweeter and quite a bit lower in alcohol. It's traditionally distilled from rice, but nowadays companies often make it from potatoes, wheat, sweet potatoes, or even tapioca. Sake and vodka are both ideal substitutes.

Makgeolli

Also spelled *makguli*, this alcoholic beverage made from fermented rice brewed with yeast has a milky appearance and is lightly carbonated; it tastes like a cross between unfiltered sake and a light wheat beer. It's often served in bowls, not unlike café au lait. You can substitute sake or white wine in recipes.

Starches

Short-Grain Rice

The standard at every Korean meal, short-grain, Korean-grown white rice is available in every Korean grocery store.

Sweet Rice (Chapssal)

Another type of short-grain rice, sweet rice (also known as glutinous rice) gets especially sticky when cooked, which is why it's referred to as glutinous although it does not actually contain gluten. It's my secret ingredient in the crunchy mung bean pancakes called *bindaetteok* (page 67).

Noodles

Korean cuisine features all sorts of noodles. The most common types include *japchae*, which are thin cellophane noodles made of sweet potato starch; *jajangmyeon,* which, much like Chinese egg noodles, are fresh and have a great chew; and buckwheat noodles, which are used often (and some varieties have added potato starch to give the noodles a bit of elasticity). Finally, there are *kalguksu,* which translates to "hand-cut," a reference to their thick, rough texture; they're made of wheat and if you can't find them, dry or fresh udon noodles make a perfect substitute.

Dried Mung Beans and Mung Bean Powder

Dried mung beans get soaked and pulverized for *bindaetteok* (page 67), which are crunchy and slightly addictive pancakes. Mung bean powder gets mixed with water and allowed to gel to form noodles for *tangpyeongchae* (page 72). Essential ingredients, both the dried beans and powder are readily available online and at Korean grocery stores.

Rice Flour

Regular rice flour is made of ground white rice, and seems to make everything it touches crisp. I can't make Seafood and Scallion Pajeon (page 151) without it.

Sweet Rice Powder

Sweet rice powder (also called sweet rice flour) is made from ground sweet rice and is a great thickener. I use it often and can't make my Ultimate Cabbage Kimchi (page 37) without it. Regular rice flour makes a good substitute.

Rice Cakes

Rice cakes, or *tteok* (pronounced "duck"), are made from ground glutinous rice. They take all sorts of shapes, from long, 1-inch-thick cylinders to small, flat, coinlike discs. They are used in savory preparations like soups and stir-fries, or are served as sweets (in all sorts of shapes) that are stuffed with red bean paste, nuts, and even jujubes. The sweet variety is often eaten at celebratory events like birthdays and weddings and is a traditional New Year's Day meal throughout Korea.

Produce

Napa Cabbage

Napa cabbage is probably the most widely used vegetable in all of Korean cuisine. It is the essential ingredient in cabbage kimchi. Be sure to buy heads that are firm and not cracked at the stem end.

Moo (White Radish)

Mco (sometimes known as *mu*) is the Korean variety of daikon radish. Larger and wider than Japanese daikon, it's got a mild, slightly sweet flavor. It's used both raw and cooked. Be sure to pick out *moo* that are smooth and have bright green tops.

Scallions and Garlic

Found in every grocery store in America, scallions and garlic inform nearly every Korean recipe.

Korean Pears

Korean pears, also known as Asian pears and Asian pear apples, are consumed widely in Korea. They're eaten on their own as a snack, are sliced into kimchi, and even ground to use as a sweetener and tenderizer in marinades.

Perilla Leaf

Perilla leaves, known as *ggaennip* in Korean and *shiso* in Japanese, are often referred to as "sesame leaves," a misnomer that comes from the taste of their seeds (see Perilla Seeds, page 10). The flavor of the leaves is a mix of wild mint, apples, sesame, and coriander. Perilla leaves are essential for wrapping up barbecued meats in *ssams* and are a delicious addition to salads and

NAPA CABBAGE

MOO

SCALLIONS

more. If you can't find them, fresh mint leaves are a good substitute.

Korean Cucumbers

Longer and thinner than typical American cucumbers, the Korean variety have thin skin and are nearly seedless. Good substitutes are European or hothouse cucumbers.

Lettuce

Red and green leaf lettuce are stacked on nearly every Korean table and are used to make *ssams* (lettuce wraps). Wrapping your protein and seasoning in lettuce is almost like having handheld salad. Great for kids!

Hallabong

The *hallabong* is a citrus fruit that grows with abandon on Korea's Jeju Island. They are very sweet, often quite large, and are distinguished by the bump at the top of each fruit, not unlike American honeybell tangerines. At home in America, I find that a combination of tangerine zest and juice well mimics the flavor of Jeju's *hallabongs*.

Mushrooms

Pyogo, also known as shiitakes, are the favorites of Korean cooks; *paengi* (enoki) are also used in many dishes.

PERILLA

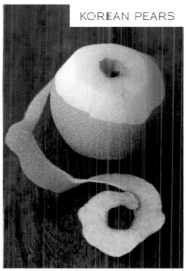

KOREAN PEARS

HALLABONG

Proteins

Pork

Pork is consumed a whole lot in Korea. Bones are boiled for broth, sliced belly is grilled and broiled and eaten with *ssamjang* (a spicy, salty condiment), chops are brushed with marinade and grilled, slices of loin and shoulder are mixed with tons of *gochujang* and garlic and stir-fried. The pig, in other words, is beloved.

Chicken

Chicken is nearly as popular as pork in Korea—boiled into soups, dipped into hot oil for unbelievable fried chicken, barbecued, and braised. Its neutral flavor is a great vehicle for the spicy and exciting flavors of Korean cooking.

Seafood

Almost completely surrounded by water, Korea offers a huge variety of fish and shellfish. Blue crabs are especially prized in the cuisine and are the main ingredient in *gejang* (page 162). Clams, oysters, sea urchin, abalone, squid, corvina, and a long silver fish known as "belt fish" are other popular choices.

Tofu

Tofu is prized in Korea. I used to think it was bland and boring, but eating it fresh in Chodang, a city known for making the best tofu in Korea, completely changed my perspective! While seasoned and smoked versions are available, the most commonly used tofu is plain and simple and either soft or firm. Extra-soft tofu is available in plastic tubes at Korean grocery stores and is the best option for dishes like *sundubu* (page 71), but the tofu available in plastic boxes at every grocery store is often quite good. If you live near an Asian market, look out for fresh tofu and give it a try.

Beef

The entire cow is put to use in Korean cooking. Bones, especially oxtails, are boiled for stock; ribeye is thinly sliced and marinated for *bulgogi*; short ribs are ground into juicy burgers, braised whole, and sliced thinly and grilled; tenderloin is chopped finely by hand for tartare; and brisket forms the base of many soups and stews.

Tools

Scissors

No Korean kitchen is complete without a few pairs of sharp scissors. They're used to cut the legs off crabs, scallions into bite-size pieces, cooked meat off the bone at family barbecues, and noodles into small strands (especially helpful for kids).

Gloves

I wear disposable plastic gloves all the time in the kitchen. It makes doing things like mixing huge batches of *gochujang* (red pepper paste) into kimchi a clean and easy project since I can really get in there and then just toss the gloves, leaving my hands clean and odor free.

Metal Chopsticks

Koreans use metal chopsticks to eat everything. They're a little slippery at first, but practice makes perfect. The best part is that they're dishwasher safe so you can use them over and over again!

Rice Cookers

If you make a lot of rice, as just about every Korean does, a rice cooker is pretty handy. It helps make perfect rice every time and it's a lot easier to clean than the burnt-on bottoms of pots.

Stone Pots

Essential for getting the heat necessary for lots of Korean dishes, heavy stone pots are a worthwhile investment, especially if you like the crispy rice at the bottom of *bibimbap* (page 177). They are used directly on the stovetop and retain heat like nothing else (which makes cast iron pans a perfect substitute). They come in various sizes ranging from small individual pots to larger ones used for communal eating. Note that you should never use soap to clean a stone pot. Simply rinse it with water.

Charcoal

Good hardwood charcoal makes a big difference if you do a lot of barbecuing. It gets hotter than hot, which helps caramelize food and will also infuse your grilled meats and more with smoky flavor.

Pots of *doenjang* fermenting in Andong

Pantry Sauces and Dressings

These are the essential seasonings that I reach for again and again. Most can be made in quantity and stored in a tightly sealed container in the refrigerator for weeks or more, to add a welcome shot of spice and depth to simple soups, salads, and grilled dishes. Mix up a batch or two and I bet you'll find yourself using them often.

UMMA PASTE

— MAKES ¾ CUP —

This heady, outspoken combination of ingredients informs many of my recipes and gives everything a loud Korean presence. I use it so often that I have named it "Umma Paste," which means "Mother Paste." I boil it into soups like *kimchi jjigae* (page 58) and use it to flavor dishes like Easy Braised Chicken (page 142).

4 large garlic cloves, peeled
3 tablespoons gochugaru (red pepper powder)
3 tablespoons fish sauce
3 tablespoons soy sauce
3 tablespoons gochujang (red pepper paste)
3 tablespoons soju

Combine all of the ingredients in a blender and puree to a smooth paste.

SPICY UMMA PASTE

This spicier version of the ubiquitous seasoning is great when you want an extra punch. Feel free to substitute it for Umma Paste in any recipe.

8 large garlic cloves, peeled
¼ cup gochugaru (red pepper powder)
3 tablespoons soju
2 tablespoons fish sauce
2 tablespoons soy sauce
¼ cup gochujang (red pepper paste)

Combine all of the ingredients in a blender and puree to a smooth paste.

SPRUCED-UP GOCHUJANG

— MAKES ⅓ CUP —

I keep this in my refrigerator at all times and my entire family eats it regularly with rice, barbecued meats, or even spread onto a sandwich for unexpected kick.

¼ cup gochujang (red pepper paste)
1 tablespoon rice vinegar
2 teaspoons toasted sesame oil
2 teaspoons roasted sesame seeds
Dash of dashida or fish sauce

Combine everything in a small bowl and whisk until combined.

SESAME OIL WITH SALT AND PEPPER

It seems silly to offer a recipe for something so simple, but accessorizing a few spoonfuls of sesame oil with a pinch of coarse salt and a few fresh grinds of pepper elevates it to favorite condiment status. It's the perfect thing to swipe pieces of *samgyeopsal* (barbecued pork belly) through before you wrap them in perilla or lettuce leaves.

JALAPEÑO SOY SAUCE

— MAKES 2 CUPS —

Every month or so I mix up a batch of this and keep it in the refrigerator. It finds its way into dipping sauces, salad dressings, and marinades where it always lends a great balance of salty and spicy.

2 cups good-quality soy sauce
4 jalapeño peppers, coarsely chopped (leave the seeds in if you love spice, discard them if you don't)

Pour the soy sauce into a glass jar. Add the jalapeños and refrigerate for at least 6 hours before using, though it keeps covered for up to a month.

KOREAN SALAD DRESSING

This flavorful, low-fat dressing adds a Korean vibe to a mundane green salad and is especially good with crunchy, interesting combinations like thinly sliced raw cabbage, shredded carrots, and thin slivers of snow peas and cucumber.

¼ cup soy sauce

2 tablespoons plus 1 teaspoon toasted sesame oil

2 tablespoons rice vinegar

1 tablespoon fish sauce

1 teaspoon red pepper flakes

1 teaspoon roasted sesame seeds

2 teaspoons Korean honey citron marmalade or orange marmalade

Combine everything in a small bowl and whisk until combined.

SCALLION DIPPING SAUCE

— MAKES 1 CUP —

I serve this with all sorts of savory pancakes and dumplings. It's even great for simple roast chicken.

½ cup good-quality soy sauce

¼ cup toasted sesame oil

2 tablespoons rice vinegar

2 tablespoons gochugaru (red pepper powder)

6 scallions, thinly sliced

Combine everything in a small bowl and whisk until combined.

김치와 반찬

KIMCHI AND BANCHAN

Sitting down to a Korean meal has a protocol unlike any other ethnic cuisine. Whether you're in a restaurant or in someone's home, it's likely that most of the real estate on the table's surface will be occupied by small dishes that are collectively known as *banchan*. Like tapas in Spain or mezes in the Middle East, *banchan* consist of small plates of flavorful food. *Banchan* are meant to be eaten with your meal, though if you finish one or two before your main dish arrives, it's typical to get free refills (it's kind of like polishing off your popcorn before the movie begins . . .).

While some *banchan* can be a bit time-consuming to prepare (long-marinated crabs, for example), most are really simple and can be made quickly. In the spirit of Korean efficiency, most home cooks will make *banchan* in large batches and serve a little bit at each meal over the course of a week. Approached this way, serving an assortment of *banchan* at each meal is entirely doable. At the same time, each type of *banchan* is so delicious on its own and most can absolutely be served as a side dish or appetizer in a more Western-style meal. The recipes in this chapter are easy and quick to prepare, making *banchan* an approachable part of any meal. The recipes are really guidelines—let seasonality, the farmers' market, and your own personal preferences inspire you.

The most typical *banchan*, actually the most typical food in all of Korea, is kimchi. In fact it's hardly considered a Korean meal without kimchi. While there are tons of different types of kimchi, piquancy ties them all together. Personally I prefer sour kimchi, which, like a good cheese, gets its flavor from age. However you like it, kimchi adds that extra hit of acid and salt everywhere it goes—it's like a squeeze of lime in a cocktail, a bit of hot pepper vinegar added to a pot of long-cooked Southern greens. While kimchi is often eaten as is alongside other foods, it's also often employed in many cooked dishes such as *kimchi jiigae* (a hit-the-spot soup that is a breeze to prepare). Using kimchi not only as a condiment but also as an ingredient is a surefire way to get tremendous flavor in a short period of time. In fact, the liquid from kimchi is even used as an important seasoning ingredient. It doesn't hurt that kimchi is one of the healthiest foods on the planet, full of good bacteria, antioxidants, fiber, and even vitamin C.

Set a Korean Table

Setting a Korean table requires a slightly different approach from a Western table setting. First and foremost, it's helpful to have as much real estate available on the table as possible, as a traditional Korean meal requires a lot of dishes! *Banchan*, the small side dishes that accompany the main dishes, are placed in the center of the table so that everyone has access to them. The main dish (or dishes) is also served communally. Each diner should have his own bowl of rice as well as a pair of chopsticks and a spoon. Most typically both the chopsticks and spoons are made of stainless steel (sturdy and reusable), but sometimes you will see these implements made of wood (especially with temple cuisine, where noise is to be avoided) and sometimes out of fancier materials, such as bronze, for special occasions.

THE ULTIMATE CABBAGE KIMCHI

— MAKES ABOUT 6 QUARTS —

This kimchi, consisting of squares of napa cabbage aggressively seasoned with red pepper and garlic and fermented with fish sauce and salted shrimp, is the most ubiquitous and recognizable and it's my personal favorite. I know it's good because my Korean mother raves about it. You can easily halve or even quarter this recipe if the quantity is intimidating, but I guarantee you'll be back for more.

Prepare the cabbage: Remove any unattractive outer leaves from the cabbages and quarter each cabbage lengthwise. Cut out and discard the cores. Cut each cabbage quarter crosswise into 2-inch pieces.

Fill your sink (you may even want to use the bathtub!) with cold water and wash the cabbage, letting any grit sink to the bottom. Lift the cabbage out of the water leaving the dirt behind and drain. Rinse out the basin and refill with fresh water. Repeat the process once more.

Get out your biggest bowls (you will have about 32 cups of chopped cabbage) and layer the cabbage with the salt so that the cabbage is evenly salted. Set aside for 45 minutes, then give the cabbage a good mix with your hands. Let it sit for an additional 45 minutes. By this point the cabbage should be quite wilted. Fill the sink (or tub) with fresh water and rinse the cabbage two times as you did earlier to remove all the salt. Drain thoroughly.

Prepare the seasoning: Place 3 cups of water in a saucepan and whisk in the rice powder. Bring to a simmer over low heat, whisking constantly, until the mixture thickens, about 3 minutes. Add the sugar and cook another minute. Take the mixture off the heat and let cool (you can speed up the cooling process by submerging the bottom of the pot in a bowl of ice water).

(recipe continues)

4 large heads napa cabbage
2 cups coarse salt
$^{1}/_{2}$ cup sweet rice powder
$^{1}/_{2}$ cup sugar
1-inch piece ginger, peeled
1 cup peeled garlic cloves
$^{1}/_{3}$ yellow onion
$^{1}/_{2}$ cup fish sauce
$^{1}/_{2}$ large white radish (moo or daikon), peeled and cut into matchsticks (about 4 cups)
2 big bunches scallions (about 20), cut into 2-inch pieces
3 cups gochugaru (red pepper powder)
$^{2}/_{3}$ cup drained Korean salted shrimp

Combine the ginger, garlic, and onion in a blender or food processor and puree until smooth. Add the fish sauce and combine thoroughly.

Prepare the kimchi: In a large bowl, combine the cooled rice powder porridge, pureed garlic mixture, radish, scallions, red pepper powder, and salted shrimp and mix well. The best way to do this is to get yourself a pair of disposable plastic gloves and use your hands.

Mix this seasoning mixture with the cabbage and pack into 6 glass quart jars or a large plastic container, being sure to pack the kimchi in tightly to press out as much air as possible. Put a sheet of plastic wrap directly on the surface of the kimchi and then cover the containers with their lids. Let the kimchi get to know itself at room temperature for 2 to 3 days depending on how sour you like it (I've even let it sit out for 4 days). After this initial fermentation, store the tightly covered kimchi for up to 6 months in the refrigerator where it will continue to ferment and improve in flavor. Always be sure to push down on the plastic to keep as much air out of the kimchi as possible.

Variation: Radish Kimchi This recipe can be easily adapted to use the large white radishes known as *moo* in Korea and *daikon* in Japan. Simply substitute julienne strips of *moo* or small whole *moo* for the cabbage and follow the same salting and seasoning (including the 4 cups of radish already called for in the seasoning) preparations. Two recipes in one!

The Anchor of Korean Cuisine

Kimchi is the cornerstone of every Korean meal. It's long been prized for its health benefits and nearly medicinal qualities; it balances and cuts rich foods, and has undeniable flavor and punch. There are over a hundred varieties of kimchi and many regional variations. Some are made from whole cabbages stuffed with baby octopus, others made solely of long chives or whole radishes.

Like sauerkraut, the cabbage is treated with salt and other flavorings and left to ferment and develop healthy bacteria, a distinctive aroma, and unbeatable taste. I love to make it in huge batches just as my Korean family does at home, because kimchi only gets better with age. If it takes up too much real estate in your refrigerator, consider giving some away to friends and family. Spread the kimchi love!

엑스트라

WATER KIMCHI

There are so many different kinds of kimchi, even one known as "bachelor kimchi" that uses small radishes with their green tops still attached, said to resemble the ponytails once typical of Korean bachelors. One of my favorite types is *dongchimi*, also known as water kimchi, a clean-tasting, refreshing kimchi made without any red pepper. Fermented with salt and sugar in plenty of water with the sweet flavors of Korean pear, scallions, and ginger, water kimchi produces not only great, crunchy vegetables, but also a flavorful liquid that becomes the base of one of my favorite cold noodle soups, Dongchimi Maemi Guksu (page 197).

Combine the cabbage and radish with 2 tablespoons of the salt in a large bowl and toss to coat. Let the mixture stand for 20 minutes. Add the pear, garlic, and scallions, and stir to combine. Pack the vegetables into 4 glass quart jars or a gallon plastic container. Meanwhile, dissolve the sugar and the remaining 4 tablespoons salt in 8 cups cold water and pour over the kimchi. Cover the kimchi and let sit at room temperature for 2 to 4 days depending on how fermented you like it. After this initial fermentation, store the tightly covered kimchi for up to a month in the refrigerator where it will continue to ferment and improve in flavor.

1 head napa cabbage, cut lengthwise into 1-inch-wide strips

$1/3$ large white radish (moo or daikon), sliced into thin 1-inch-wide, 2-inch-long rectangles (about $1^1/_2$ cups)

6 tablespoons coarse salt

1 Korean pear, peeled and sliced into thin half-moons

6 garlic cloves, peeled and halved

6 scallions, cut into 2-inch pieces

2 tablespoons sugar

JEAN-GEORGES'S FAST, HOT KIMCHI

— SERVES 4 TO 6 —

Kimchi is very personal and is all about your particular preferences. This is my husband's version, which is to say it's quick kimchi for the impatient. It is delicious and is great with grilled or broiled fish, shellfish, chicken, or pork.

2 tablespoons gochujang (red pepper paste)

2 tablespoons sherry vinegar

2 tablespoons fish sauce

2 tablespoons grapeseed or canola oil

1 small red onion, thinly sliced

1 teaspoon perilla seeds

1 teaspoon coriander seeds

1 tablespoon gochugaru (red pepper powder)

1 head napa cabbage, coarsely chopped, core discarded

1 small Korean pear, peeled, cored, and coarsely diced

1 Korean cucumber (or ½ hothouse cucumber, seeded), coarsely chopped

Whisk together the red pepper paste, vinegar, and fish sauce in a small bowl.

Heat the oil in a large wok over high heat. Add the onion, perilla seeds, coriander seeds, and red pepper powder. Cook until the onion begins to brown, about 1½ minutes.

Pour the red pepper paste mixture over the onion, stirring to combine. Cook for 1 minute, until the liquid is nearly evaporated, then immediately stir in the cabbage, pear, and cucumber. Cook until the cabbage is wilted and the flavors are nicely combined, about 5 minutes. Taste and season with additional vinegar or fish sauce if you think it needs it.

SPICY MARINATED PEARL ONIONS

This is essentially two recipes in one since the combination yields not only delicious, slightly pickled onions that are the perfect accompaniment for rich foods like fried chicken, but also the most incredibly flavored liquid that is delicious spooned over grilled meats or even raw fish. While peeling fresh pearl onions is labor-intensive, I think it's worth it since you get a great crunch. (Frozen pearl onions work well too, even though they're slightly softer.)

3 cups peeled pearl onions
2 jalapeño peppers, thickly sliced (see Note)
1½ cups soy sauce
¾ cup rice vinegar

Combine all of the ingredients in a 1-quart jar or container and cover tightly. Let the mixture sit at room temperature, stirring now and then to keep all of the onions submerged, for up to 3 days. Transfer to the refrigerator, where they will keep for up to 2 months.

Note: I use the chile pepper's seeds since I like the onions to be quite spicy, but feel free to discard them if you like tamer onions.

SAUTÉED CARROTS AND BUTTERNUT SQUASH

— MAKES ABOUT 2 CUPS —

Grating vegetables that normally take a long time to cook speeds up the process tremendously. This grate-and-sauté method can be used with any hard vegetable including parsnips, beets, and turnips. This can be successfully served hot out of the pan, at room temperature, or even cold.

Heat the vegetable oil in a large nonstick skillet over medium-high heat. Add the garlic and ginger and cook until fragrant, about 30 seconds. Add the carrots and squash and continue to cook, stirring now and then, until just tender and cooked through, about 8 minutes.

2 tablespoons vegetable oil

1 garlic clove, minced

1-inch piece fresh ginger, finely minced

3 carrots, coarsely grated (about 1 cup)

1 cup coarsely grated butternut squash

SAUTÉED SPINACH

— SERVES 4 TO 6 AS A SIDE DISH —

Using lots of garlic and soy sauce instead of salt gives this very typical spinach preparation a Korean bent. Try it out with any leafy green.

Heat the oil in a large saucepan over medium-high heat. Add the garlic and cook until fragrant, about 30 seconds. Add the spinach and stir to coat it with the garlicky oil. Cook just until the spinach is wilted, about $1\frac{1}{2}$ minutes. Remove from the heat and drizzle with the soy sauce. Serve hot or chilled.

2 tablespoons vegetable oil

2 garlic cloves, thinly sliced

6 cups baby spinach leaves

1 teaspoon soy sauce

FRESH BEAN SPROUT SALAD

The method for this salad—tossing a crunchy vegetable with a quick, Korean-inspired dressing—can be used for just about any *banchan*. Try it with shredded cabbage (almost like a Korean-German coleslaw), sliced cucumbers, or matchsticks of zucchini.

2 cups fresh mung bean sprouts

2 teaspoons vegetable oil

2 teaspoons toasted sesame oil

2 teaspoons rice vinegar

$\frac{1}{4}$ teaspoon gochugaru (red pepper powder)

Pinch of sugar

Pinch of coarse salt

$\frac{1}{2}$ teaspoon roasted sesame seeds

Bring a pot of water to a boil, add the sprouts, and cook just until beginning to soften, less than a minute. Drain the sprouts in a colander and place in a bowl of ice water or rinse under cold running water to stop them from cooking.

Meanwhile, whisk together the vegetable oil, sesame oil, vinegar, red pepper powder, sugar, and salt in a bowl. Add the sprouts to the bowl and stir to coat with the dressing. Taste for seasoning and sprinkle with the sesame seeds. Serve immediately if you like it quite crunchy or let it sit covered in the fridge for up to a day if you prefer it a bit more wilted. Either way, serve the salad cold.

ROASTED SWEET POTATOES WITH SESAME SAUCE

— MAKES ABOUT 2 CUPS —

This ridiculously simple sauce tastes good on just about anything, especially rich vegetables like sweet potatoes. It would be equally good with cubes of steamed or roasted kabocha squash or, for something lighter, blanched asparagus.

Preheat the oven to 400°F. Line a baking sheet with parchment paper.

Toss the cubes of sweet potato with the oil and spread on the baking sheet in a single layer. Sprinkle with salt and roast, stirring now and then, until browned and a paring knife easily pierces through the potatoes, about 15 minutes.

Meanwhile, whisk together the tahini and boiling water, thinning with more water if the sauce is too thick. Season to taste with salt.

Drizzle the warm sweet potatoes with the sauce and serve. The sweet potatoes can also be served at room temperature.

2 cups cubed (1/2-inch) sweet potato (from about 1 large, peeled sweet potato)

1 tablespoon vegetable oil

Coarse salt

2 tablespoons tahini (sesame seed paste)

1 tablespoon boiling water

KOREAN SLAW

¼ cup packed brown sugar

Grated zest and juice of 2 limes

2 tablespoons rice vinegar

1 teaspoon coarse salt

2 cups white radish matchsticks

2 cups shredded napa cabbage

1 carrot, cut into matchsticks

4 scallions, thinly sliced

1 small Korean pear, peeled and cut into matchsticks

1 cup jicama matchsticks

1 small red onion, thinly sliced

¼ cup chopped cilantro

1 tablespoon roasted sesame seeds

This slaw was devised by Joseph Lee for his Bulgogi Tacos (page 84). Not only is it the fresh, crunchy note that sets his tacos over the edge, it's also a delicious salad served as a side dish or as a *banchan*.

In a large bowl, whisk together the brown sugar, lime zest and juice, vinegar, and salt. Add the radish, cabbage, carrot, scallions, pear, jicama, red onion, cilantro, and sesame seeds and toss well to combine. Let the slaw sit for at least 15 minutes before you eat it. Taste for seasoning and add more sugar, vinegar, or salt if you think it needs it.

KOREAN CHOPPED SALAD

— SERVES 6 —

4 tomatoes, chopped

4 cucumbers, coarsely chopped

3 scallions, thinly sliced

6 large perilla leaves or 12 fresh mint leaves, slivered

¼ cup olive oil

2 tablespoons soy sauce

2 teaspoons gochugaru (red pepper powder)

½ teaspoon coarse salt

This impromptu recipe was devised by Julia Turshen, my collaborator on this book, as a way to use up ingredients left over after we shot the cooking segments for *Kimchi Chronicles*! Turns out this crunchy salad goes well with just about anything—grilled fish, roasted shrimp, even next to a turkey sandwich.

Stir together the tomatoes, cucumbers, scallions, and perilla leaves in a large bowl. Whisk together the oil, soy sauce, red pepper powder, and salt in a small bowl. Pour the dressing over the salad and toss to combine.

COLD BROCCOLI SALAD

— SERVES 4 —

This cool, crunchy salad of barely cooked broccoli tossed with a light, flavorful dressing is the perfect make-ahead dish; it only gets better as it sits in the fridge. Cooking the garlic in the oil for the dressing doesn't just impart great flavor, it also leaves you with addictive garlic chips that make an unexpected garnish.

Bring a pot of water to a boil. Add the broccoli and cook just until bright green, less than a minute. Drain the broccoli and chill in a bowl of ice water or rinse under cold running water to stop the cooking process.

Meanwhile, heat the olive oil and garlic in a small pan over medium heat. Cook just until the garlic is golden brown, 1 minute, and use a slotted spoon to transfer the garlic slices to a paper towel–lined plate. Whisk the warm garlic oil together with the sesame oil, vinegar, soy sauce, and sugar in a large mixing bowl. Add the blanched broccoli and stir to combine. Serve garnished with the garlic chips.

4 cups broccoli florets
3 tablespoons extra-virgin olive oil
1 garlic clove, thinly sliced
1 teaspoon toasted sesame oil
1 tablespoon rice vinegar
1 teaspoon soy sauce
Pinch of sugar

SCALLION SALAD

A quick and simple *banchan*, this refreshing salad goes well with all barbecued foods and is especially good tucked into a lettuce leaf with pork or beef. If you want to make this a really speedy dish, buy already shredded scallions from the produce department of your local Korean grocery store. You can also use a large yellow onion thinly sliced into half-moons.

Place the scallions in a large bowl. Whisk together the remaining ingredients in a small bowl and pour over the scallions. Toss to combine. That's it.

1 bunch scallions, shredded
1 teaspoon gochugaru (red pepper powder)
1 teaspoon fish sauce
1 ½ teaspoons toasted sesame oil
2 teaspoons rice vinegar

SEAWEED WITH GARLIC AND VINEGAR

Sometimes when I make dishes like Birthday Seaweed Soup (page 57), I get overeager with the amount of dried seaweed I soak before cooking it. Instead of wasting it, I came up with this quick, yummy salad. I use wakame, but use any type you prefer.

Soak the seaweed in cold water to cover for 10 minutes.

Meanwhile, whisk together the garlic, vinegar, oil, salt, sugar, red pepper powder, and black pepper in a large bowl.

Drain the seaweed, coarsely chop, and add it to the bowl with the garlic dressing. Stir to thoroughly combine. Serve at room temperature or chilled. It will keep covered in the fridge for up to 3 days.

2 large handfuls dried seaweed
2 garlic cloves, minced
2 tablespoons rice vinegar
2 tablespoons vegetable oil
Pinch of coarse salt
Pinch of sugar
Pinch of gochugaru (red pepper powder)
Pinch of freshly ground black pepper

야채와 두부

VEGETABLES AND TOFU

Korean cuisine is like a playground for vegetarians. It offers so many dishes packed with great flavor, texture, and substance that you probably wouldn't notice the absence of meat unless someone pointed it out. Some of my favorite food moments in Korea include biting into the satisfying crunch of *bindaetteok* (a pancake made completely out of mung beans) and the terrific contentment of scraping the bottom of the bowl after a big serving of *sundubu jjigae* (a hearty, spicy tofu-based stew).

A highlight of any trip to Korea is visiting vegetarian restaurants—and also the vegetable markets, where women sitting on stools use small knives to peel their wares and proffer samples. I've had the good fortune to visit Chodang, the capital city of tofu. Located near the coast and right next to Lake Gyeongpo, Chodang is *the* place to go for fresh tofu. Distinguished by the combination of fresh water, salt water, and local soybeans, Chodang's tofu tastes simultaneously of the earth, the sea, and the lake—no small feat for something often considered the definition of "bland." When I was there I got to see tofu being made in the traditional fashion, which includes soaking and manually grinding homegrown soybeans. I found the process to be quite similar to cheese making.

Later I got to try four superb tofu dishes. The first was *biji*, made from the pulp that's left over once the ground beans are strained, served with soy sauce and rice. It's got a nutty flavor and a texture similar to grits and really shows the virtues of avoiding waste during production (in fact, the owner of the restaurant uses the

leftover water from the tofu-making process as detergent—he swears by it!). I also had amazing *sundubu jjigae*, a simple dish of fresh tofu with soy sauce and scallions that made me appreciate the beauty and simplicity of fresh tofu, and a very soft tofu dish served cold and seasoned with a bit of salty ocean water. It was an incredible meal that made me appreciate a familiar ingredient in so many new ways.

I also had a memorable meal at Sanchon, a restaurant in Seoul that serves temple cuisine. I learned that certain vegetables, like garlic and scallions, are forbidden in temple cuisine because of their strong aromas. The absence of aromatic seasonings didn't, surprisingly, produce bland food; on the contrary, my meal at Sanchon included an exciting variety of dishes such as beautiful wild herbs served simply dressed, a delicious fried mushroom served with persimmon vinegar, and crunchy vegetable pancakes. I spoke with Yon-Shik Kim, the monk who runs the restaurant, about his cooking and he explained that there is really something special about temple cuisine, something nearly magical. Nothing is obscured and every dish tastes completely of what it is. I found the food inspiring in its clarity.

This chapter includes not only traditional Korean recipes like the *bindaetteok* and *sundubu jjigae*, but also vegetarian recipes suited to the American kitchen, including two addictive corn dishes from Jean-Georges. He developed the dishes in the late summertime in New York when corn is at its best and our Korean pantry inspired the terrific pairing of *gochugaru*'s (red pepper powder) spicy heat with corn's picked-at-its-peak sweetness.

BIRTHDAY SEAWEED SOUP

— SERVES 4 TO 6 —

Seaweed soup is a traditional birthday dish in Korea. It's eaten in homage to mothers who are encouraged to eat the soup before they give birth since seaweed is so healthy and does all sorts of good things for both mother and child: It offers a big dose of calcium for strong bones; iodine, which helps to regulate the thyroid; and lots of magnesium too. This soup is not only easy to make, it's totally comforting, especially when served with rice and kimchi.

Soak the seaweed in cold water to cover for 10 minutes, drain well, and coarsely chop.

Meanwhile, heat the sesame oil in a large, heavy pot over high heat. Add the brisket and season with salt and pepper. Cook, stirring now and then, until browned on all sides, about 3 minutes.

Add the seaweed and garlic and stir to combine. Add cold water to cover, bring to a boil, and skim any foam that rises to the surface. Add the fish sauce (or *dashida*) and cook at a rolling boil until the seaweed is quite soft and the broth has taken on lots of flavor, 45 minutes to 1 hour.

2 large handfuls of dried seaweed, such as wakame

2 tablespoons toasted sesame oil

$1/3$ pound beef brisket, thinly sliced

Coarse salt and freshly ground black pepper

8 garlic cloves, minced (garlic is your friend!)

2 teaspoons fish sauce or dashida

KIMCHI JJIGAE (KIMCHI STEW)

Jjigae is the Korean word for stew, and let me tell you—I'm the *jjigae* lady. I love to make *jjigaes*, and *kimchi jjigae* is one of the easiest to make (I can't imagine it's a coincidence that it's one of the most regularly consumed dishes in all of Korea). It's the absolute best way to use up your oldest, most sour kimchi, an example of the Korean tendency to be extremely resourceful and to never throw anything away. In Seoul we went to a cool barbecue restaurant called Saemaul Shikdang that's known for its "7-Minute Jjigae," which takes exactly 7 minutes to prepare. I cook mine a bit longer, but I think the flavor is still pretty impressive.

2 tablespoons toasted sesame oil

1 pound pork belly, cut into ¼-inch dice

Coarse salt and freshly ground black pepper

½ large yellow onion, coarsely chopped

3 cups coarsely chopped kimchi with a bit of its liquid (use the most pungent, sour kimchi available for best flavor)

1 tablespoon fish sauce or dashida

1 slice American cheese (optional)

5 scallions, thinly sliced

About ¼ cup thinly sliced gim (see Note), for garnish

Heat the sesame oil in a large soup pot over medium heat. Add the pork belly, season with salt and pepper, and cook, stirring now and then, until rendered, browned, and crispy, about 10 minutes.

Add the onion and kimchi and stir to combine. Add enough water to nearly cover the pork mixture (5 or 6 cups), cover, and bring to a boil. Immediately reduce the heat and simmer until the onion and kimchi are softened and the soup is quite thick, about 20 minutes.

Stir in the fish sauce (or *dashida*), American cheese (if using), and scallions. If it's too thick for your liking, thin the stew with water. Cover the pot and simmer for 10 minutes to combine the flavors. Serve steaming hot sprinkled with *gim*.

Note: *Gim* is pressed and toasted sheets of laver seaweed. Japanese nori makes a good substitute.

KIMCHI JJIGAE WITH TUNA

This even faster variation of *kimchi jjigae* is a favorite of my Korean family's and is ideal for those who don't eat meat. Use the most pungent, sour kimchi available for best flavor.

2 tablespoons toasted sesame oil

5 cups kimchi

½ yellow onion, cut into thin half-moons

1 can (5 ounces) oil- or water-packed tuna, drained

1 tablespoon Umma Paste (page 23)

½ slice American cheese

6 scallions, cut into 1½-inch pieces

Combine 4 cups water, the sesame oil, kimchi, onion, and tuna in a large heavy pot. Bring to a boil over high heat, cover, and cook at a vigorous boil for 10 minutes.

Add the Umma Paste and cheese, reduce the heat to low, cover, and cook for 5 minutes to blend the flavors. Add the scallions, cover again, and cook until they're just wilted, 4 to 5 minutes.

All the American Cheese?

You'll notice a few very American, very not-Korean ingredients in lots of my recipes. For example, American cheese is used to thicken and flavor jigaes. I add soda pop to the marinades for *galbi* and *bulgogi* to lend sweetness and a tenderizing effect. Hot dogs get dressed with kimchi and sliced into stews. Even peanut butter is stirred into broths. A lot of these foods found their way into pantries in Korea after American GIs rationed them to Koreans during the war; a lot of them also got incorporated into traditional dishes by Korean-Americans who learned to adapt to the available ingredients. I think Koreans might just have put the "K" in Kraft...

해스티라

DOENJANG JJIGAE (SOYBEAN PASTE STEW)

— SERVES 4 —

Think of this as miso soup fit for a football player. Unlike a refined Japanese preparation of miso with perhaps a little slice of scallion or a perfect cube of tofu bobbing on top, this is packed with meat, shellfish, and vegetables and it's all supported by a flavorful, *doenjang*-enhanced broth. If you're feeling weak, this stew will definitely make you stronger!

2 tablespoons toasted sesame oil

$^1/_2$ pound beef brisket, cut into $^1/_2$-inch dice

Coarse salt

$^1/_3$ cup doenjang (soybean paste); see Note

$^1/_4$ cup Umma Paste (page 23)

4 potatoes (about 2 pounds total), peeled and diced

2 small yellow onions, coarsely chopped

2 cups coarsely diced zucchini

1 container (14 ounces) firm tofu, cut into 1-inch cubes

1 dozen small hardshell clams, such as littlenecks or Manila, scrubbed

4 large shell-on shrimp

4 scallions, thinly sliced

Cooked rice and kimchi, for serving

Heat the sesame oil in a heavy soup pot over medium heat. Add the beef, season with salt, and cook, stirring now and then, until just browned on all sides, about 2 minutes. Add 8 cups water and bring the soup to a boil, skimming off any foam that rises to the surface. Stir in the *doenjang* and the Umma Paste and cook the soup at a rolling boil for 10 minutes.

Add the potatoes, onions, zucchini, and tofu. Cover the pot and cook at a boil until the potatoes can be easily pierced with a paring knife, about 20 minutes.

Add the clams and shrimp, cover, and cook just until the clams are opened and the shrimp are bright pink, about 2 minutes. Serve the stew hot, sprinkled with scallions and with rice and kimchi on the side.

Note: Some people find the coarse texture of *doenjang,* with its small pieces of soybean, a bit too rustic. I love it, but if you prefer a more refined texture, simply push the *doenjang* through a fine strainer before using it.

TOFU WITH SOY SAUCE, SCALLIONS, AND SESAME SEEDS

— SERVES 4 —

Understated and elegant, this is also the simplest dish ever, so the quality of the ingredients is critical. Good tofu and soy sauce, crispy scallions, and roasted sesame seeds make a difference. It's worth seeking out fresh tofu if you can find it for the most refined flavor—most Asian grocery stores will stock it, and if you live in a big city like New York or San Francisco, look around Little Korea or Chinatown for local purveyors.

Arrange the tofu on a platter. Drizzle with the soy sauce, then sprinkle evenly with the scallions and sesame seeds. Serve at room temperature.

1 pound best-quality (fresh if possible) soft tofu, cut into 1-inch cubes

2 tablespoons soy sauce

2 scallions, thinly sliced

2 teaspoons roasted sesame seeds

DOORE TOFU (LEMONS STUFFED WITH TOFU AND NUTS)

— SERVES 4 —

Acknowledging the delicacy of fresh tofu, chef Sook Hee of Seoul's Doore restaurant served us tofu paired with citrus and nuts in this almost yogurtlike presentation. It's completely representative of Sook Hee's cooking style—simple, stunning, old school, but with such a light touch and distinctive, unmuted flavors. Jean-Georges loved this tofu dish and when he lifted the citrus to smell it, that small inquisitive gesture showed Sook Hee immediately that he too has a passion for food. Jean-Georges has since re-created this tofu dish at home using both lemons and tangerines and we love to serve it as a light appetizer or even a predessert dessert.

Prepare the lemons by first trimming off and discarding a small slice from the peel at the bottom of each fruit so that they easily stand up. Then trim ½ inch off the top of each fruit and set the tops aside. With a sharp paring knife, cut in between the spongy white pith and the flesh of each lemon, taking care not to cut through the peel at the bottom or sides. With a small spoon, scoop out the pulp (and set aside), leaving the shells intact. Squeeze 2 tablespoons of lemon juice from the pulp (and hold on to the rest of the pulp in case you need more juice later).

Coarsely chop the ⅓ cup peanuts and the pine nuts in the food processor. Add the sugar, honey, salt, tofu, and the 2 reserved tablespoons lemon juice. Pulse the mixture until just combined. Taste and add more sugar, salt, or lemon juice if you think it needs it.

Divide the pureed tofu mixture evenly among the lemon shells. Top each serving with a small pinch of the finely chopped peanuts, pistachios, red pepper powder, chives, and an edible flower (if using). Set the reserved tops on each lemon and serve.

4 lemons

⅓ cup salted roasted peanuts, plus 2 teaspoons finely chopped for garnish

1 tablespoon pine nuts

1 teaspoon sugar

1 teaspoon honey

¼ teaspoon coarse salt

½ of a 14-ounce container soft tofu

2 teaspoons finely chopped pistachios

Large pinch of gochugaru (red pepper powder)

2 tablespoons baby chives or chopped chives

4 edible flowers (optional)

MRS. RHEE'S BINDAETTEOK (MUNG BEAN PANCAKES)

Bindaetteok look quite a bit like latkes and are very similar to falafel, but instead of being deep-fried balls of ground chickpeas (or fava beans), *bindaetteok* are flat cakes made with ground dried mung beans, water, and a little seasoning and shallow-fried until super crispy. I was only able to perfect them after taking advice from my friend Eric's mother. A great home cook, Mrs. Rhee recommended adding a bit of sweet rice to the mung beans, which is the secret ingredient that makes them really hold together and also helps to produce a caramelized crust. While this recipe is all about the kimchi, you could omit the kimchi and the kimchi liquid to make a plain pancake (simply add another $1/2$ cup water to the batter). You can also add chopped pork belly to the batter instead of, or in addition to, the kimchi.

Combine the mung beans and rice in a medium bowl. Add cold water to cover by at least 1 inch and soak for at least 6 hours and up to 24.

Drain the soaked mung beans and rice and place in a blender along with $1/2$ cup fresh water, the kimchi liquid, fish sauce, sesame oil, soy sauce, and salt. Blend just until smooth, being careful not to overmix (it should be coarsely pureed as opposed to perfectly smooth). Transfer the mixture to a large bowl and fold in the kimchi.

Heat a thin layer of vegetable oil in a large nonstick skillet over medium-high heat. Using a $1/4$-cup measure, ladle in the pancake batter to form 4 pancakes and cook until crisp and browned on the first side, about 2 minutes. Carefully flip and cook until crisp and browned on the second, about 2 minutes. Transfer the pancakes to a paper towel–lined plate and continue with the remaining batter and more oil as necessary. Serve hot with Scallion Dipping Sauce.

2 cups dried mung beans, rinsed in a few changes of cold water

$1/4$ cup sweet rice, rinsed in a few changes of cold water

$1/2$ cup sour kimchi liquid

1 teaspoon fish sauce

1 teaspoon toasted sesame oil

1 teaspoon soy sauce

Pinch of coarse salt

1 generous cup finely diced sour kimchi

Vegetable oil, for frying

Scallion Dipping Sauce (page 27)

Street Food

Many of my favorite Korean dishes come from street carts and stands where some of the best and most beloved food in Korea can be found. In Seoul's Namdaemun Market the amazing food stalls include a few places where you can get the best *galchi jorim* (a dish of braised fish and *moo*). In Gwang-Jang Market, one of Korea's largest and oldest traditional markets and perhaps the best place to eat Korean street food, there's a nearly dizzying collection of vendors who make all sorts of incredible food, inducing traditional beef tartare, hundreds of varieties of kimchi, and mouthwatering *bindaetteok*. Insadong Market, something like Seoul's SoHo, has stands and carts selling everything from *tteok* (rice cakes) to silkworm larvae and Dragon's Beard candy made of stretched honey and nuts (it tastes like a PayDay candy and it's one of my favorite things to bring back to friends as a gift). It turns out Korea is a great place to eat standing up.

My husband went crazy for the street food in Korea, as he does in all of Asia. In fact, he spent over 2 weeks traveling all around Asia eating only street food right before he opened his restaurant Spice Market, where the menu is composed entirely of street food–inspired dishes. His best tip is to eat from vendors who are near schools, as they often have the most nostalgic food (not to mention the most hygienic). Areas near temples and churches also tend to attract good vendors. Luckily in Korea everyone eats street food and it's a very safe thing to do—the health code and water quality standards are high and well maintained.

I've been making these *bindaetteok* practically every weekend since tasting them at the market.

SUNDUBU JJIGAE (SPICY VEGETABLE AND TOFU STEW)

— SERVES 6 TO 8 —

Sundubu jjigae is a healthy, spicy stew that elevates tofu from basic to exciting. In this stew, the base of dried anchovies (a magic seasoning) and kelp (which has got major umami flavor) lend a tremendous depth of flavor for very little effort. It's a great example of the efficient beauty of Korean food—you can have a developed, strong stock ready in just 20 minutes. Jean-Georges "wow'ed" this soup when I first made it, always a good sign.

Bring 3 quarts of water to a boil in a large soup pot. Place the anchovies and kelp in a metal sieve and lower into the water. Simmer for 20 minutes to fully infuse the water with lots of flavor. Remove and discard the anchovies and kelp.

Add the shiitakes, leek, zucchini, onion, chile, and Umma Paste. Cover and boil until the vegetables are quite soft, about 15 minutes. Add the watercress and tofu, return to a boil, and cook until the watercress is completely wilted and the tofu is heated through, about 5 minutes. Just before serving, add the scallions and ladle into big bowls. Serve piping hot garnished with baby or torn watercress.

Note: You could also substitute 2½ containers (14 ounces each) soft tofu, drained and broken into large pieces.

20 dried anchovies, heads and innards discarded

One 6-inch square dried kelp

6 large fresh shiitake mushroom caps, thickly sliced

1 large leek, white and pale green parts only, coarsely chopped

2 small zucchini, diced

1 yellow onion, diced

1 spicy-but-not-too-spicy green chile pepper, thinly sliced

Umma Paste (page 23)

1 large handful of watercress, stems and leaves torn into 1½-inch pieces

3 containers (11 ounces each) extra-soft tofu, broken into large pieces (see Note)

6 scallions, thinly sliced

Baby watercress or an additional small handful of torn watercress, for garnish

TANGPYEONGCHAE (MUNG BEAN JELLY NOODLES WITH VEGETABLES)

— SERVES 4 TO 6 —

Sang-Ok Choi is the 73-year-old founder of Yongsusan, the famed restaurant that's expanded to eight branches in Korea, and a ninth in Los Angeles. Her success is truly remarkable given she was 53 when her first restaurant opened. With its North Korean influence, Choi's food is milder and lighter than most of the Korean food Americans are familiar with. This doesn't mean her food is boring; in fact, the meal Jean-Georges and I had at Yongsusan in Seoul was one of our favorites; her *tangpyeongchae* (mung bean jelly noodles) were particularly impressive. The noodles themselves are all about texture—they are virtually flavorless. When combined with beautiful, fresh vegetables and a nicely balanced dressing, they make for a transcendent dish.

½ **cup mung bean powder**

2 **tablespoons vegetable oil**

1 **egg, lightly beaten**

6 **fresh shiitake mushrooms, caps only, thinly sliced**

⅓ **cup soy sauce**

2 **teaspoons rice vinegar**

2 **tablespoons gochugaru (red pepper powder)**

2 **scallions, thinly sliced**

1 **garlic clove, minced**

½ **cucumber, cut into strips**

½ **cup white radish (moo or daikon) matchsticks**

5 **red radishes, thinly sliced**

2 **teaspoons slivered fresh ginger**

1 **handful of mung bean sprouts**

In a saucepan, stir 3½ cups cold water into the mung bean powder. Set the pan over medium-high heat and cook, stirring, until the mixture thickens and becomes nearly translucent, 3 or 4 minutes. Pour the mixture into a loaf pan. Let cool at room temperature until completely solidified, about 1 hour.

Heat 1 tablespoon of the oil in a nonstick skillet over medium-high heat. Add the egg, tilting the pan so the egg covers the surface in as thin a layer as possible. Cook until it's just set, about 1 minute, then carefully flip the omelet over and cook for another minute. Slip the omelet onto a plate and let it cool.

Add the remaining 1 tablespoon oil to the same pan and heat over medium-high heat. Add the mushrooms and cook, stirring now and then, until browned and softened, about 6 minutes. Set aside. Slice the cooled egg omelet into thin ribbons and set aside.

Turn the mung bean jelly out of the loaf pan onto a cutting board. Cut the jelly crosswise into thin slices as if it were a loaf of bread, then cut each slice lengthwise into noodles.

In a large bowl, whisk together the soy sauce, vinegar, red pepper powder, scallions, and garlic. Add the mung bean noodles, cucumber, radishes, ginger, and sprouts to the bowl and toss gently to combine. Garnish the noodles with the reserved egg ribbons and shiitakes.

EASY CORN PUDDING WITH KOREAN RED CHILE AND LIME

— SERVES 6 GENEROUSLY —

This is a by no means a traditional Korean dish—it uses American corn and is baked in the oven. But the pairing of sweet, summer corn with the fruity spice of Korean red chile is a heavenly match. Jean-Georges loves this technique of coarsely grating the corn and baking the mixture, a sort of fresh polenta with a concentrated corn flavor—pretty brilliant.

7 tablespoons unsalted butter

1 dozen ears of corn, shucked

2 tablespoons fresh lime juice

$\frac{1}{2}$ teaspoon gochugaru (red pepper powder), plus a pinch for garnish

1 teaspoon coarse salt

Preheat the oven to 400°F.

Rub 1 tablespoon of the butter over the surface of a 10-inch cast iron pan. Grate the corn on the coarse side of a box grater into the prepared pan, being sure to get all the pulp and milk. Bake the corn for 20 minutes, or until it's a bit puffed, a lot of the moisture has evaporated, and the top has a light crust.

Remove from the oven and mix in the remaining 6 tablespoons butter, the lime juice, $\frac{1}{2}$ teaspoon red pepper powder, and salt. Taste for seasoning, adding more salt, red pepper powder, or lime as necessary. Serve sprinkled with an extra pinch of red pepper powder.

GRILLED CORN WITH MAYONNAISE AND GOCHUGARU

— SERVES 6 —

Another recipe that highlights the killer corn-and-chile combination, this one is a virtual snap to assemble. It's a Mexican-Korean hybrid that would be perfect with Joseph's Bulgogi Tacos (page 84).

Preheat a grill to high or preheat a ridged cast iron grill pan over high heat. Brush the corn with the oil and place on the hot grill. Cook, turning now and then, until lightly charred on all sides, 5 to 6 minutes. Sprinkle the hot corn with salt, brush with the mayonnaise, and dust with some red pepper powder.

6 ears of corn, shucked
2 tablespoons vegetable oil
Coarse salt
¼ cup mayonnaise
Gochugaru (red pepper powder)

코리안 바베큐

KOREAN BARBECUE

The tradition of barbecue in Korea is particularly fascinating and is perhaps the most popular style of Korean food in America. Like the American barbecue tradition, which is regionally specific (meaty beef ribs and brisket in Texas, juicy pulled pork in North Carolina, dry rubs in Memphis, etc.), Koreans are exacting and thoughtful when it comes to putting meat on a fire. The two most popular barbecue dishes are *samgyeopsal* (barbecued pork belly) and *galbi* (barbecued sliced short ribs). While *samgyeopsal* requires nothing but the best-quality meat you can find and an appreciation for pork fat, *galbi* is often marinated before cooking. Each region—in fact, each family—favors a slightly different marinade, but almost everyone uses lots of soy sauce and garlic.

In this chapter I've offered not only a great recipe for *galbi*, but also lots of different barbecued dishes with sauces and marinades that range from the spicy to the sweet, from the garlic-laden to the onion-packed. Mix and match and experiment and I'm sure you'll find, as I have, that Korean ingredients like *gochujang* and sesame oil make interesting and welcome additions to your grilling routine.

Another interesting component of Korean grilled dishes is *ssams*, or wraps. These stretch out a small amount of grilled meat or even boiled and grilled pork belly (for the famous dish *bo ssam*) to feed a crowd, and the layering of lettuce, rice, and meat with other flavorings like grilled garlic cloves, perilla leaves, *ssamjang* (a condiment that is basically a mixture of *gochujang* and *doenjang*), and kimchi

results in a fresh, healthy meal that's engaging and fun to eat. It's also a great way to introduce children to Korean food.

Korean barbecue isn't limited to meat and poultry. Fish and shellfish are often prepared over hot coals. In fact, one of my favorite places to eat seafood when I'm in Korea is in the northern city of Sokcho, where most of my family lives, at Byulmi Gui Restaurant (the name literally translates to "delicacy grilling"). The restaurant is located in Daepo, an amazing port and outdoor seafood market that's lined with stalls filled with local specialties, including fried shrimp, simply grilled whole fish, which are wrapped in napkins and taken to go (roe and all), and pan-fried slices of stuffed squid. Byulmi Gui consists of little tables with built-in grills and pairs of gloves for each table so that customers don't need to hesitate when handling hot clam and scallop shells. The mollusks are placed whole onto the grills and removed once they open (the *pop pop pop* sound of the shells is like music), and they're eaten in large amounts, bigger pieces cut to a more manageable size with scissors. The immaculately fresh seafood becomes infused with smoky flavor but doesn't dry out since it steams in its own juice inside the shells. Bites are dipped into *gochujang* that's served in empty shells, and the buckets for shells under the tables keep everything in order. It's all so simple and ingenious, and it's absolutely the inspiration behind the Mixed Seafood Grill with Korean Chile Butter (page 98).

GRILLED STEAK WITH KIMCHI BUTTER

— SERVES 4 —

David Chang is a Korean-American chef who runs the Momofuku restaurant empire in New York City. To say he's a big deal is an understatement. His restaurants have been visited and recognized by just about everyone. His food is by no means distinctly Korean; it's influenced by Japan and Korea, as well as the American South, France, and of course New York. David's Korean heritage, though, remains a loud voice in the chorus of all of these cultures. Kimchi, for example, comes up in different guises all over his menus, and his kimchi butter is so delicious that it's tempting to eat it just on its own. Influenced by David, this simple compound butter makes ordinary grilled steak unforgettable.

Using a fork, mash the butter with the kimchi and kimchi liquid until thoroughly combined. Place the butter on a large piece of plastic wrap and form into a log, using the plastic to help you. Refrigerate the butter for at least 1 hour before using (although you can store it for up to 1 week tightly wrapped).

Preheat a grill to high or preheat a ridged cast iron grill pan over high heat. Sprinkle the steaks on both sides with the red pepper powder and plenty of salt and black pepper. Drizzle both sides with the sesame oil. Grill about 4 minutes per side (depending on the thickness) for medium-rare. Transfer the steaks to a cutting board, cover loosely with foil, and allow the steaks to rest for at least 5 minutes.

To serve, cut the butter into 4 coins. Top each steak with a coin of butter and serve immediately, letting the butter melt over the steaks.

4 tablespoons salted butter, at room temperature

3 tablespoons finely chopped kimchi, plus 1 tablespoon kimchi liquid (use the sourest kimchi available for best flavor)

4 ribeye steaks ($\frac{1}{2}$ pound each) or 2 pounds of any steak you prefer

2 teaspoons gochugaru (red pepper powder)

Coarse salt and freshly ground black pepper

2 tablespoons toasted sesame oil

LA GALBI (THINLY SLICED BARBECUED SHORT RIBS)

— SERVES 4 —

It's not entirely clear why this version of *galbi* (short ribs) is called LA Galbi, but the general consensus is that it's because the meat for *galbi* is cut differently in Korea than it is in America—specifically in Los Angeles, which has the largest concentration of Koreans in this country. "LA-style" short ribs are sliced thin, which allows the marinade to really penetrate; they are also cross-cut so that each slice includes a bit of bone, which, incidentally, makes for a nice little handle. It's typical to make *ssams*, or wraps, by rolling the grilled meat in lettuce leaves with some spicy peppers and a bit of *ssamjang*—a Korean condiment that's essentially a mix of *gochujang* (red pepper paste) and *doenjang* (soybean paste). If you want to be really Korean use scissors to cut the cooked meat off the bones.

Rinse the short ribs being sure to brush off any fragments of bone that might remain. Pat dry.

Combine the onion, pear, garlic, ginger, sugar, pepper, soy sauce, soda, and soju in a blender and puree until completely smooth. Transfer the mixture to a bowl, add the short ribs, sesame seeds, and scallions and turn to coat with the mixture. Cover the bowl and marinate in the refrigerator overnight.

Preheat a grill to high or preheat a ridged cast iron grill pan over high heat. Remove the meat from the marinade. Grill the *galbi* until cooked through and nicely caramelized on both sides, about 1 1/2 minutes per side. Transfer to a large platter along with the *ssam* fixings and wrap away.

Note: If you can't find "LA-style" short ribs, ask your butcher to thinly slice short ribs for you.

2 1/2 pounds beef short ribs cut "LA-style" (see Note)

1/4 yellow onion, chopped

1/4 Korean (Asian) pear, peeled and coarsely chopped

6 garlic cloves, peeled

1 tablespoon chopped ginger

1/4 cup sugar

1/2 teaspoon freshly ground black pepper

1/2 cup soy sauce

1/2 cup cola

1/4 cup soju, sake, or vodka

1 1/2 teaspoons roasted sesame seeds

2 scallions, thinly sliced

Ssam fixings: Red or green leaf lettuce leaves, perilla leaves, rice, sliced hot green chile peppers, and ssamjang

JOSEPH'S BULGOGI TACOS

— SERVES 4 (MAKES 1 DOZEN TACOS) —

Joseph Lee, a young Korean-American guy who lives in New York and hails from Philadelphia, is a great musician and, it turns out, an astoundingly good home cook who makes pretty spectacular Korean tacos. Chef Roy Choi, the man behind the popular Kogi Korean BBQ-To-Go trucks and spin-off restaurants, started the Korean taco trend in Los Angeles. Joseph's version includes his signature *bulgogi*, a Korean-inspired slaw, an ingenious Korean-Mexican red sauce, Mexican *crema*, and the most textural topping—a sprinkle of ground wasabi peas and ground chicharrones (fried pork skins). It's a lot of elements, but each one is really simple to make and the sum of all the parts is one of the best tacos around.

BULGOGI

$^1/_2$ teaspoon coarse salt

$^1/_4$ teaspoon freshly ground black pepper

$^1/_4$ teaspoon ground cinnamon

$^1/_4$ teaspoon ground cumin

1 pinch of grated nutmeg

2 tablespoons brown sugar

1 can (12 ounces) Coca-Cola

$^1/_2$ cup soy sauce

2 tablespoons rice vinegar

1 tablespoon toasted sesame oil

Worcestershire sauce

1-inch piece fresh ginger, cut into thin coins

3 garlic cloves, smashed

$^1/_3$ yellow onion, sliced

1 pound ribeye steak, sliced nearly paper thin (see Note)

KOREAN-MEXICAN RED SAUCE

1 bay leaf

Coarse salt and freshly ground black pepper

1 vine-ripened tomato

$^1/_3$ yellow onion

$^1/_2$ red bell pepper

3 garlic cloves, peeled

$^1/_4$ cup gochujang (red pepper paste)

1 tablespoon roasted sesame seeds

2 teaspoons toasted sesame oil

1 teaspoon soy sauce

$^1/_4$ teaspoon ground cumin

TACOS

1 dozen corn tortillas

2 cups Korean Slaw (page 48)

$^3/_4$ cup Mexican crema (or $^1/_2$ cup sour cream whisked with $^1/_4$ cup water)

$^1/_3$ cup wasabi peas, finely ground in a food processor

$^1/_3$ cup chicharrones, finely ground in a food processor

To start the bulgogi: Whisk together the salt, black pepper, cinnamon, cumin, nutmeg, brown sugar, Coca-Cola, soy sauce, vinegar, sesame oil, and a few dashes of Worcestershire sauce in a large bowl. Add the ginger, garlic, and onion to the marinade. Add the meat and nestle in among the ginger, garlic, and onion slices. Cover the bowl and allow the meat to marinate for at least 30 minutes at room temperature or up to overnight in the refrigerator.

To make the Korean-Mexican red sauce: Bring a saucepan of water to a boil. Add the bay leaf, a pinch of coarse salt, a few grinds of pepper, the whole tomato, piece of onion, bell pepper, and garlic cloves. Boil the vegetables until they're totally soft, about 15 minutes.

Discard the bay leaf and use a slotted spoon to transfer the vegetables to a blender. Add 2 tablespoons of the cooking water, the red pepper paste, sesame seeds, sesame oil, soy sauce, and cumin to the vegetables and blend until completely smooth. Season to taste with salt and pepper and thin with a bit more of the cooking water if needed (the final consistency should be like pancake batter).

To finish the bulgogi: Preheat a grill to high or preheat a ridged cast iron grill pan over high heat.

When you're ready to eat, remove the meat from the marinade and grill it until caramelized on both sides, about 1 minute per side. If you'd like, you can wrap the pieces of ginger, garlic, and onion from the marinade (including a bit of the marinade) in foil and let it cook on the back of the grill (these little pieces make a great snack for the cook).

To assemble the tacos: Warm the tortillas for 20 seconds in the microwave or heat on your hot grill or grill pan. Fill each one with a few slices of grilled *bulgogi*, a few spoonfuls of slaw, a drizzle of *crema*, a drizzle of red sauce, and a sprinkle of both the ground wasabi peas and the ground chicharrones.

Note: Presliced ribeye steak is sold in Korean grocery stores as *bulgogi*. In a non-Korean store, ask your butcher to slice it for you. Or if that isn't an option, put the steak in the freezer for 30 minutes (to make it easier to cut) and then slice it as thinly as possible with your sharpest knife.

HOT DOGS WITH KIMCHI RELISH

— SERVES 4 —

In this recipe, my most favorite American street food gets a makeover for the Korean palate. Jean-Georges created a kimchi relish that's made sweet with honey and sour with rice vinegar. All you need is a baseball game and you're good to go.

½ cup kimchi, thinly sliced

2 teaspoons honey

2 teaspoons rice vinegar

4 hot dogs

4 hot dog rolls

4 tablespoons Korean hot mustard

Preheat a grill to high or preheat a ridged cast iron grill pan over high heat.

Mix together the kimchi, honey, and vinegar in a small bowl.

Grill the hot dogs until browned and crispy, and lightly grill the rolls until they're golden brown. Put the hot dogs in the rolls and top each one with 1 tablespoon mustard and one-quarter of the kimchi relish.

GRILLED PORK CHOPS WITH SPICY BARBECUE SAUCE

Grilled pork chops are an easy way to get dinner on the table. This spicy barbecue sauce, which takes about 1 minute to make, shifts pork chops from mundane to finger-licking-good.

Fire up your charcoal grill in two zones (one with coals and one without) or preheat a grill to high or preheat a ridged cast iron grill pan over high heat.

Whisk together the red pepper paste, ginger, garlic, honey, soy sauce, red pepper powder, and salt in a medium bowl. Brush the pork chops all over with the sauce.

Reduce the grill to medium-high (or if you're working on a charcoal grill, move over to the indirect side) and grill the chops on both sides until firm to the touch and nicely glazed, 10 to 15 minutes. Let them rest for 5 minutes before serving.

¼ cup gochujang (red pepper paste)

1 tablespoon finely grated fresh ginger

2 garlic cloves, finely grated

2 tablespoons honey

4 teaspoons soy sauce

2 teaspoons gochugaru (red pepper powder)

½ teaspoon salt

4 double-cut pork loin chops

Where There's Smoke...

Since each table in each barbecue restaurant in Korea has its own built-in grill, the restaurants have learned how to deal with a tremendous amount of smoke. Above every table you'll find a metal smoke collector, an exhaust tube that comes down from the ceiling and can be placed close to the cooking food to essentially vacuum every bit of smoke generated—an efficient and smart solution.

BO SSAM (PORK BELLY WITH TOPPINGS)

— SERVES 4 TO 6 —

Traditionally *bo ssam* is simply boiled and sliced pork belly, but grilling the boiled slices is a terrific variation that provides the contrast of crispy fat with soft, yielding meat. Although the array of suggested traditional toppings might seem a bit random, eaten all together it's a surprisingly well-balanced combination.

Preheat a grill to high or preheat a ridged cast iron grill pan over high heat. Grill the pork belly slices on both sides until browned and crispy on the outside, about 1 minute per side.

The classic way to eat *bo ssam* is to top a lettuce leaf with a perilla leaf and then a piece of pork. Dab the pork with *ssamjang*, add a little of the kimchi, a tiny bit of salted shrimp, an oyster (why not?), and a bit of Scallion Salad. Wrap the whole thing into a bundle and eat bent at the waist, since it's guaranteed to be a delicious mess.

2 pounds boiled pork belly (from pork belly stock, page 135), cut into ⅓-inch-thick slices

1 bunch red or green leaf lettuce leaves

1 dozen perilla or shiso leaves

About ½ cup ssamjang

1 cup radish kimchi, store-bought or homemade (page 38)

¼ cup Korean salted shrimp, drained

1 dozen freshly shucked oysters

Scallion Salad (page 51)

TTEOKGALBI (SEASONED SHORT RIB BURGERS)

— SERVES 4 —

Tteokgalbi, essentially Korean hamburgers, actually originated as royal court cuisine, but I treat these as weekend, at-home food for my family. These are especially great served alongside Grilled Corn with Mayonnaise and Gochugaru (page 75).

1½ **pounds ground short ribs (see Note)**

1 **tablespoon finely minced garlic**

1 **teaspoon finely grated fresh ginger**

3 **tablespoons grated Korean (Asian) pear**

2 **scallions, thinly sliced**

2 **tablespoons soy sauce**

1 **tablespoon sugar**

½ **tablespoon toasted sesame oil**

1 **teaspoon roasted sesame seeds**

½ **teaspoon coarse salt**

½ **teaspoon freshly ground black pepper**

Preheat a grill to high or preheat a ridged cast iron grill pan over high heat.

Use your hands to gently mix together all of the ingredients just enough to combine and form into 4 burgers. Grill to desired doneness.

Note: If you can't get find ground short ribs or your butcher won't grind them for you, you can substitute ground chuck with at least 20% fat. Or you can buy short ribs on the bone and easily grind them at home in the food processor. For 4 burgers, purchase at least 3 pounds of bone-in short ribs. Cut all the meat off the bone and cut off and discard any large pieces of fat. Coarsely chop the meat with your knife and then pulse it in small batches in the food processor. The secret is the small batches so that the meat just gets chopped and doesn't turn into a paste.

SPICE-RUBBED KOREAN CHICKEN

— SERVES 4 —

This dry-rub mixture is the greatest balance of salt, sweet, and heat. A big batch of it packed into a glass jar would be the perfect hostess gift since it lasts forever and is incredibly versatile. Here it's used to pack a heavy hit of flavor onto chicken breasts, but it would work equally well on a slowly braised pork shoulder or even a rack of ribs.

Whisk together the soy sauce, vinegar, and oil in a large bowl. Add the chicken breasts and turn to coat with the marinade, then cover the bowl and refrigerate for at least a half hour and up to overnight.

Preheat a grill to high or preheat a ridged cast iron grill pan over medium heat. Carefully oil the hot grates or pan (use a brush or an oil-saturated paper towel folded in quarters) to prevent sticking.

Meanwhile, mix together the sugar, red pepper powder, salt, and pepper in a small bowl. Pat the chicken breasts dry and rub evenly with the spice mixture.

Grill the chicken until firm to the touch and completely cooked through, about 4 minutes per side depending on their thickness. Let the breasts rest for a few minutes before slicing thinly on the bias.

2 tablespoons soy sauce

1 tablespoon rice vinegar

¼ cup vegetable oil, plus more for cooking

4 boneless, skinless chicken breasts

2 teaspoons sugar

2 teaspoons gochugaru (red pepper powder)

1 teaspoon coarse salt

1 teaspoon black pepper

BARBECUED CHICKEN WITH SWEET BARBECUE SAUCE

— SERVES 4 TO 6 —

This barbecue sauce, made sweet with Korean honey citron marmalade, gets nice and sticky as it cooks on the chicken. Serve with lots of napkins! It's also really nice served with grilled eggplant. Just slice the eggplant, salt it, brush it with olive oil, and grill it alongside the chicken. Season with salt and pepper when it's hot. Yum.

¼ **cup gochujang (red pepper paste)**

2 tablespoons toasted sesame oil

3 tablespoons gochugaru (red pepper powder)

½ **cup Korean honey citron marmalade or orange marmalade**

¼ **cup soy sauce**

2 tablespoons soju, sake, vodka, or water

2 tablespoons fish sauce

8 garlic cloves, finely minced

One 4-pound chicken, cut into 10 pieces (2 wings, 2 drumsticks, 2 thighs, breasts halved), or 5 legs divided into thighs and drumsticks

Whisk together the red pepper paste, sesame oil, red pepper powder, marmalade, soy sauce, soju, fish sauce, and garlic in a large bowl. Add the chicken, stir to coat, and marinate in the refrigerator for at least 2 hours or up to overnight.

Fire up your charcoal grill in two zones (one with coals and one without) or preheat a grill to medium or preheat a ridged cast iron grill pan over medium heat. Grill the chicken (on the indirect side if you're using a charcoal grill), turning now and then, until it is firm to the touch (or until an instant-read thermometer registers 165°F—smaller pieces will be done before larger ones), about 10 minutes for the wings, 15 for the breasts, and 20 minutes for the legs and thighs.

GRILLED CHICKEN SANDWICH WITH ASIAN PEAR AND BIBIMBAP MAYONNAISE

— SERVES 4 —

Jean-Georges kept sneaking spoonfuls of the sauce from my *bibimbap* (page 177), so I finally had to give him my recipe. He transformed it into a delicious sandwich spread that is put to good use on this simple chicken sandwich that would be a hit in any lunchbox. When he made these with our neighbor Hugh Jackman, it was then decided that Hugh's epitaph will be: "Generous with the mayonnaise."

Preheat a grill to high or preheat a ridged cast iron grill pan over high heat. Rub the chicken with the oil and sprinkle evenly with salt. Grill until firm to the touch and cooked through, 3 to 4 minutes per side, depending on the thickness. Set the chicken aside.

Whisk together the red pepper paste, mayonnaise, sesame oil, vinegar, and sesame seeds. Spread both sides of the buns with the sauce. Put the chicken on the bottom halves of the buns, top with some pear and greens, and sandwich with the top halves of the buns. Go to town.

4 boneless, skinless chicken breast halves (about 5 ounces each)

2 tablespoons olive oil

Coarse salt

3 tablespoons gochujang (red pepper paste)

2 tablespoons mayonnaise

1 tablespoon toasted sesame oil

2 teaspoons rice vinegar

3 tablespoons roasted sesame seeds, coarsely ground with a mortar and pestle

4 sesame seed buns, toasted

$\frac{1}{4}$ cup peeled Asian pear matchsticks

Small basil or mint leaves, or shredded lettuce

MIXED SEAFOOD GRILL WITH KOREAN CHILE BUTTER

— SERVES 6 —

Things move fast in Korea. My friend April pointed out that you often hear people shouting, "*ppal-li, ppal-li*" meaning "hurry, hurry." Daepo-Hang, the port area in the city of Sokcho, is emblematic of the fast-paced, seemingly impatient scene. Fishermen sell their catch, motorcycle and scooter riders push through the crowds, people pop in and out of shops and stop at stands to enjoy quick snacks like fried shrimp. When I was in the area with my friend Diana we had the most delicious, simply grilled shellfish—clams and scallops set straight onto the grill and eaten with *gochujang*. When I told Jean-Georges about the experience, he improvised a similar meal in our backyard, adding some lobster and shrimp (why not?) and transforming the *gochujang* into a wonderfully balanced butter with a bit of lime, too.

1 cup (2 sticks) unsalted butter

¼ cup gochujang (red pepper paste)

¼ cup soy sauce

¼ cup fresh lime juice

3 lobsters, halved lengthwise

2 dozen large shell-on shrimp

2 dozen littleneck clams, scrubbed

Fire up your charcoal grill or preheat a grill to high heat or preheat a large, ridged cast iron griddle, straddled over two burners, over high heat.

Melt the butter in a small saucepan. Whisk in the red pepper paste, soy sauce, and lime juice and keep warm.

Place the lobsters shell-side down on the grill and drizzle the flesh side with some of the butter. Set the shrimp and clams directly on the grill. Flip the shrimp when they're bright pink on the first side and take them off the grill when they're fully cooked on the second side, 5 to 6 minutes. When the clams open, spoon a bit of the butter into them; the clams should be opening by the time the shrimp are done. And by the time you get the clams and shrimp off the grill, the lobsters should be done. All in all, everything will take about 15 minutes.

Put any remaining butter in a bowl to dip the shrimp in as you peel them.

EMO'S GRILLED SQUID

Emo is the Korean word for "aunt." When I was last in Sokcho, my *emo*, who used to run a restaurant, cooked a feast on the beach for my entire Korean family. We had a spicy crab soup, grilled pork belly and grilled vegetables, boiled octopus, kimchi brought from home, and this simple grilled squid dish with an impromptu sauce. The meal, however, went way beyond the food. It was about being with family, about being in the place where you come from, and feeling welcome and part of something bigger than yourself. Families not only define cultures, they transcend them—we are all connected to our homes and origins, wherever they are and however we define them. I make this dish at home sometimes and it always brings me back to that special afternoon.

2 garlic cloves, finely minced

2 tablespoons toasted sesame oil

1 tablespoon rice syrup or honey

1 teaspoon gochugaru (red pepper powder)

$\frac{1}{2}$ teaspoon freshly ground black pepper

$\frac{1}{4}$ cup gochujang (red pepper paste)

2 pounds whole small squid, cleaned

2 teaspoons roasted sesame seeds

Preheat a grill to high or preheat a ridged cast iron grill pan over high heat.

Whisk together the garlic, sesame oil, rice syrup, red pepper powder, and black pepper in a small bowl.

In a large bowl, whisk together the red pepper paste and 2 tablespoons of water and add the squid, tossing to coat. Grill the squid until firm and opaque, about $1\frac{1}{2}$ minutes a side. Transfer the squid to a platter (you can serve them whole or cut up with scissors into bite-size pieces). Serve drizzled with the reserved garlic-sesame sauce and sprinkled with the sesame seeds.

Throw a Korean Picnic

Koreans love to cook and eat outdoors—so much so that camping stoves are sold in neighborhood grocery stores all around the country. I had my most memorable picnic on the beach in Sokcho (see recipe on the opposite page). In order to throw a proper Korean picnic, besides your nearest and dearest, you've got to include:

1. Real charcoal for the barbecue pit.
2. Precooked Korean rice. I swear by it!
3. Lots of bottled water, trash bags, sunscreen, and a roll of paper towels.
4. A few good blankets.
5. A list of your family's favorite songs to sing.
6. Cold beer—no need for a corkscrew!

GRILLED STUFFED SQUID

— SERVES 4 TO 6 —

I first had a version of this dish from a street vendor in the city of Sokcho. It's a traditional North Korean preparation. A very large squid was stuffed and steamed, then cut into inch-thick slices and pan-fried. When I came home to New York, I fooled around with the stuffing and simplified the recipe by stuffing small squid and throwing them on the grill. The stuffing would also be tasty inside of mushroom caps and then run under the broiler.

Heat the 2 tablespoons oil in a skillet over medium-low heat. Add the zucchini, onion, carrot, garlic, and jalapeño and cook, stirring now and then, until softened, about 10 minutes.

Combine the sautéed vegetables, rice, red pepper paste, fish sauce, soy sauce, red pepper powder, and sweet rice powder in a large bowl and toss well to coat. Allow the mixture to cool.

Stuff each squid with about 2 tablespoons of the vegetable and rice mixture (you want them to be stuffed but not bursting).

Preheat a grill to high or preheat a ridged cast iron grill pan over high heat. Brush the stuffed squid and the reserved tentacles with a little oil and sprinkle with salt. Grill until marked on the first side, 1 to 2 minutes. Carefully turn and cook until marked and browned on the second side and the squid is opaque throughout, another 1 to 2 minutes. Serve hot.

2 tablespoons vegetable oil, plus more for grilling

1 small zucchini, very finely diced

1 yellow onion, very finely diced

1 small carrot, finely diced

3 garlic cloves, finely minced

1 jalapeño pepper, seeded and finely diced

1 cup cooked white rice

1 tablespoon gochujang (red pepper paste)

1 tablespoon fish sauce

2 teaspoons soy sauce

2 teaspoons gochugaru (red pepper powder)

1 tablespoon sweet rice powder

1 dozen small squid, cleaned, tentacles removed and reserved

Coarse salt

GRILLED KOREAN LOBSTER ROLLS WITH SCALLION MAYONNAISE

— SERVES 4 —

Jean-Georges reinterpreted this classic New England sandwich using the Korean ingredients in our pantry. The lobster salad would work equally well with boiled shrimp and the scallion mayonnaise would be welcome on just about any sandwich.

Whisk together the scallions, red pepper powder, vinegar, sesame oil, salt, and mayonnaise in a large bowl.

Preheat a grill to high or preheat a ridged cast iron grill pan over high heat. Grill the lobster tails shell-side down until the flesh is just barely firm to the touch and opaque, about 8 minutes. Turn over and cook for another minute. Set the lobster aside until cool enough to handle, then shell and coarsely chop the meat.

Butter the hot dog buns generously and grill until crispy and golden brown.

Add the lobster meat to the bowl with the scallion mayonnaise and toss to coat. Pile the mixture into the toasted buns.

Note: Jean-Georges likes to use Kewpie mayonnaise for this dish. Kewpie is a Japanese brand worth finding, but regular mayonnaise works just as well.

$1/3$ **cup thinly sliced scallions**

$1/2$ **teaspoon gochugaru (red pepper powder)**

2 teaspoons rice vinegar

1 teaspoon toasted sesame oil

1 teaspoon coarse salt

5 tablespoons mayonnaise (see Note)

4 lobster tails, split in half lengthwise

4 tablespoons unsalted butter

4 hot dog buns

GRILLED SCALLOPS WITH GREEN TEA

— SERVES 4 —

This recipe makes use of green tea powder, which smells and tastes almost like ground seaweed and has a terrific grassy flavor. Be sure your grill is really hot before you add the scallops, or they will dry out before getting beautiful brown grill marks.

8 sea scallops, halved horizontally
Coarse salt
Gochugaru (red pepper powder)
Toasted sesame oil
1 lime
Green tea powder

Preheat a grill to high or preheat a ridged cast iron grill pan over high heat.

Thread 2 scallop halves onto each of 8 small bamboo skewers. Season the scallops on both sides with salt and red pepper powder and drizzle lightly with sesame oil. Grill the scallop skewers until just marked, 20 to 30 seconds on the first side. Carefully turn the skewers and cook until marked on the second side, another 20 to 30 seconds. The scallops should be nicely browned and slightly firm to the touch. Squeeze the lime over the cooked scallops and drizzle with a tiny bit of fresh sesame oil. Top each scallop with a small pinch of green tea powder.

WHOLE GRILLED BASS WITH MAKGEOLLI AND DOENJANG

— SERVES 4 TO 6 —

Sea bass with miso is a classic restaurant dish. Being a classic restaurant guy, my husband took cues from his time in Korea and reinvented the dish so it has a new Korean personality, substituting *doenjang*, coarse Korean miso paste, for traditional Japanese miso paste and thinning it out with *makgeolli*, a Korean rice ale. While a whole fish is impressive and surprisingly easy to cook, this marinade would work just as well on filets.

Cut diagonal slashes into the flesh on both sides of the fish and arrange in a large, shallow dish. Whisk together the *doenjang*, vinegar, soy sauce, sesame oil, *makgeolli*, shallots, and ginger. Pour over the fish, making sure to get the marinade into the slashes. Cover and marinate for at least 20 minutes at room temperature and up to 6 hours in the refrigerator.

Preheat a grill to medium-high or preheat a ridged cast iron grill pan over medium-high heat. Place the fish on the grill, brush with some of the marinade, and grill until browned and crisp on the first side and the flesh is easily pierced with a paring knife, 7 to 10 minutes, depending on thickness. Carefully turn the fish and baste with more of the marinade. Grill on the second side until the flesh is easily pierced with a paring knife, another 7 to 10 minutes. Transfer the fish to a large pan or platter, let them rest for at least 5 minutes. Serve sprinkled with the scallions.

- 2 whole black sea bass or striped bass (about $1\frac{1}{2}$ pounds each)
- 3 tablespoons doenjang (soybean paste)
- 3 tablespoons rice vinegar
- 1 tablespoon soy sauce
- 1 tablespoon toasted sesame oil
- $\frac{1}{2}$ cup makgeolli, sake, white wine, or water
- 2 tablespoons finely diced shallots
- 2 tablespoons finely chopped fresh ginger
- 5 scallions, thinly sliced

고기와 가금류

MEAT AND POULTRY

eef, pork, and chicken are the building blocks of simple Korean braises and quick stir-fries, of fortifying stews and soups made with boiled bones, and of course, of crispy fried deliciousness. In fact, I could happily live on Korean-style fried chicken alone. Aside from that personal addiction, meat and poultry fit healthfully into the Korean diet and are seen as components of meals and are not usually front and center. With a balanced approach to eating, Koreans have always accompanied protein with vegetables, kimchi, and rice.

Traditionally, beef has always been the most highly regarded meat in Korean cuisine. Historically, cows have been valued tremendously in Korean culture. There's even a holiday that honors cattle on the "first cow day" of each lunar new year. This high esteem, interestingly, usually meant beef wasn't widely consumed.

It has actually only gained the popularity it enjoys today in the last fifty years or so and is currently eaten often in favorite dishes like flavorful *bulgogi*, hearty braised short ribs, and the elegant, raw preparation known as *yukhoe*.

Chicken and pork are also very central to Korean cooking. Ever resourceful and economical, Korean cooks, in restaurants and at home, have traditionally used every part of both animals in many dishes. It's common to find grilled chicken hearts and skin served with drinks and entire birds that fortify and flavor soups like the famous medicinal cure-all known as *samgyetang*. Pork similarly gets put to use in all sorts of ways, and not a single part is wasted—necks go into one of my favorite stews flavored with perilla leaves and seeds (page 135) and pork belly goes into soup pots, on barbecues, and in frying pans all over the country.

BEEF TARTARE

— SERVES 4 —

Beef tartare, or *yukhoe*, is a popular dish in Korea. Jennifer, an American friend who lives in Seoul and knows more about Korean food than most Koreans, took me to a stall in Gwangjang market that's known for its tartare. The stall is called Jamejip, which means "sisters' shack," as it is owned by two sisters. Their spot has been open for over 30 years. Minja Kim, the older sister, has been making this dish for 40 years, while her younger sister, Okhee Kim, has been making it for 27 years. Seasoned gently with soy sauce and sesame oil, this tartare is an elegant and unexpected appetizer. The pine nut and Korean pear garnish not only adds great texture, but helps to make this a distinctly Korean dish. The raw egg yolk isn't just there to gild the lily, it binds everything together and offers great richness. Just be sure to buy the best-quality meat from a reputable butcher when you make this at home.

2 tablespoons pine nuts

10 ounces highest quality beef tenderloin, cold

1 tablespoon soy sauce

1 tablespoon toasted sesame oil

2 teaspoons honey

1 garlic clove, finely minced

A few grinds of black pepper

1/3 Korean (Asian) pear, peeled and cut into matchsticks

1 large organic egg yolk

Place a heavy skillet over medium heat and add the pine nuts. Cook, stirring now and then, until fragrant and lightly browned, about 2 minutes. Transfer the nuts to a plate and set aside.

Finely dice the beef using your sharpest knife. Alternatively, you can coarsely chop the beef and then pulse it in a food processor, taking care not to turn it into a paste.

Whisk the soy sauce, sesame oil, honey, garlic, and pepper together in a large bowl. Add the beef and stir to coat. Transfer the beef to a serving platter and garnish with the reserved pine nuts and Korean pear. Gently place the egg yolk in the center of the dish and serve immediately, with diners mixing everything up as they eat.

MOOGUK (RADISH AND BRISKET SOUP)

— SERVES 4 TO 6 —

This soup yields a ton of long-cooked flavor in a surprisingly short time and with very few ingredients. Healthy and economical, it's really a vegetable soup that's flavored with a small amount of meat and the roasted taste of sesame oil. My daughter, who's quite a picky eater, loves this soup and often has it for dinner alongside a bowl of steamed white rice.

Heat the sesame oil in a large heavy soup pot over medium-high heat. Add the meat along with a pinch of salt and a few grinds of pepper. Cook, stirring now and then, until just browned on all sides, about 1 minute. Add the radish and garlic and enough water to cover. Bring to a rolling boil over high heat. Reduce the heat to medium-low and skim off any foam that rises to the surface. Add another pinch of salt and the *dashida,* cover the pot, reduce to a simmer, and cook for 40 minutes.

Add the scallions to the soup, cover, and cook until the scallions are soft, about 10 minutes. Season to taste with additional salt and pepper and serve hot.

3 tablespoons toasted sesame oil

$\frac{1}{2}$ pound beef brisket, cut across the grain into $\frac{1}{4}$-inch-thick slices

Coarse salt and freshly ground black pepper

1 large white radish (moo or daikon), peeled and cut into $\frac{1}{2}$-inch cubes (about 4 cups)

3 garlic cloves, chopped

1 tablespoon dashida or fish sauce

1 bunch scallions, cut into 2-inch pieces

Chodang Elementary School

I was lucky enough to get to visit Chodang Elementary School in the city of Chodang, South Korea, to get a taste of what Korean kids eat for lunch. I was struck by the clean, efficient kitchen run by quick-moving, kind-eyed lunch ladies. The kids get their fresh, healthy food and sit at long tables with stools attached. When everyone has been served, they all cheer "Jal muk get supmida," which basically means "I appreciate this" or "Thank you for this meal"—a kind, respectful gesture representative of the Korean approach to eating. On the day I visited, the kids had rice, a clear broth with beef and radish, kimchi, a squid and bean sprout salad with gochujang, and a few rolls made of battered, deep-fried noodles and carrots wrapped in seaweed. The teachers eat the same food—kimchi for everyone! On my way out I met two young boys. One told me that they are best friends because "He understands me. We can share what's in our hearts." It was such a sweet, adult answer. When I asked the other boy why they were best friends he told me it's because "We are the same height." Ha!

BULGOGI (MARINATED THINLY SLICED BEEF)

— SERVES 4 —

Bulgogi means "fire meat" in Korean, a reference to the temperature at which it is cooked, not the spice. It's common to serve the meat with grilled whole cloves of garlic and small, spicy green peppers, as well as lots of leafy lettuce, perilla leaves, rice, and a dish of *ssamjang* to make *ssams* (lettuce wraps) just like with LA Galbi (page 83).

3 dried shiitake mushrooms

¼ cup soy sauce

¼ cup soju, sake, vodka, or other spirits

¼ cup cola

3 tablespoons sugar

¼ Korean (Asian) pear, peeled and coarsely chopped

¼ yellow onion, coarsely chopped, plus 1 small yellow onion, thinly sliced

6 garlic cloves, peeled

½ teaspoon freshly ground black pepper

4 tablespoons toasted sesame oil

1 tablespoon roasted sesame seeds

1½ pounds ribeye steak, sliced nearly paper thin (see Note)

Combine the dried shiitakes and hot water to cover in a small bowl and set aside until softened, about 10 minutes. Drain, discard the tough stems, and thinly slice the caps.

Combine the soy sauce, *soju*, soda, sugar, pear, chopped onion, garlic, black pepper, and 2 tablespoons of the sesame oil in a blender and puree until smooth. Transfer the puree to a large bowl and stir in the sesame seeds, mushrooms, sliced onion, and steak slices. Cover tightly with plastic wrap and marinate in the fridge for at least 30 minutes or up to 4 hours.

When you're ready to eat, heat the remaining 2 tablespoons sesame oil in your largest skillet over high heat. Working in batches (so as to not crowd the pan and so the meat develops delicious, caramelized edges), add the beef and marinade and cook, stirring now and then, until cooked through, 4 to 5 minutes.

Note: Presliced ribeye steak is sold in Korean grocery stores as *bulgogi*. In a non-Korean store, ask your butcher to slice it for you. Or if that isn't an option, put the steak in the freezer for 30 minutes (to make it easier to cut) and then slice it as thinly as possible with your sharpest knife.

BRAISED SHORT RIBS WITH PUMPKIN

— SERVES 6 —

When we were first served this dish at Doore, our favorite restaurant in Seoul, we just went nuts for it. While Jean-Georges has been making short ribs for years, after eating Sook Hee's version he took the French tradition of braising meat to a new place by seasoning it with Korean flavors. The result is the most ideal thing to eat in cold weather. While it's festive to eat the stew out of the pumpkins just as Sook Hee served hers, regular old bowls can, of course, be substituted

Place the short ribs, celery, carrot, shiitake caps, garlic, ginger, thyme, cinnamon sticks, kelp, allspice, stock, wine vinegar, and soy sauce in a large heavy pot. Bring to a boil, reduce to a low simmer, cover and cook until the meat is tender and nearly falling off the bone, about 3 hours. (Alternatively, cover the pot and bake in a 375°F oven for 3 hours.)

Remove the ribs to a platter and set aside until they're cool enough to handle. Strain the cooking liquid through a fine-mesh sieve into a bowl. With a ladle, carefully skim off and discard as much fat as you can from the cooking liquid. You will be left with the most delicious sauce. Set the sauce aside.

Meanwhile, trim off and discard a small slice from the bottom of each pumpkin so that they easily stand up. Trim the top 1 inch off the pumpkins and set the tops aside. Remove and discard the seeds from each pumpkin.

Bring a large pot of water to a boil. Boil the pumpkins until the flesh is just tender, about 15 minutes. Remove with a slotted spoon and set aside upside down to drain and cool.

(recipe continues)

6 whole beef short ribs

2 celery stalks, chopped

1 carrot, coarsely chopped

6 fresh shiitake mushrooms, stems removed

1 whole head garlic, halved horizontally

2-inch piece fresh ginger

Handful of fresh thyme sprigs

4 cinnamon sticks

4-inch square dried kelp (dasima or kombu)

1 tablespoon allspice berries

4 cups chicken or beef stock

2½ cups dry red wine

¼ cup red wine vinegar

3 tablespoons soy sauce

6 small pumpkins

2 cups cubed butternut squash

1 cup pearl onions

½ cup dried Korean dates (daechu or jujubes)

1 cup peeled cooked chestnuts (see Note)

Freshly ground black pepper

2 tablespoons pine nuts

Add the butternut squash cubes and pearl onions to the boiling water and cook until just tender, about 5 minutes. Meanwhile, place the dried dates in a heatproof bowl. Drain the butternut squash and onions, reserving 2 cups of the cooking water. Pour the 2 cups hot cooking water over the jujubes and set them aside to soften for 10 minutes. Drain and reserve the jujubes.

Back to the short ribs. Remove the bones from the short ribs (they should just slip out) and coarsely chop the meat, discarding any large pieces of fat. Return the meat to the pot and add the strained and defatted sauce, the butternut squash, pearl onions, chestnuts, and jujubes. Bring the stew to a boil, reduce the heat to a simmer, and cook for 15 minutes. Season to taste with black pepper.

Divide the stew among the pumpkins. Sprinkle with pine nuts, replace the pumpkin tops, and serve hot.

Note: You can cook fresh chestnuts and peel them, or use store-bought vacuum-packed cooked and peeled chestnuts that come in jars.

Doore

My first meal at the restaurant Doore ended with chef Sook Hee singing traditional Korean music unaccompanied and with great confidence and emotion. It literally left me in tears. The experience was soulful and connected. Sook Hee originally studied dance before pursuing a career in food and it's clear that her creative side motivates everything she does. An artist who thinks of the plate as a canvas, Sook Hee sees harmony among ingredients. When my husband arrived in Korea with our daughter, Chloe, I practically took them straight from the airport to Doore. Jean-Georges too was blown away by the experience, and so appreciative of Sook Hee's talent and grace. He instantly recognized her as an extraordinary embodiment of Korean cuisine and culture.

엑스트라

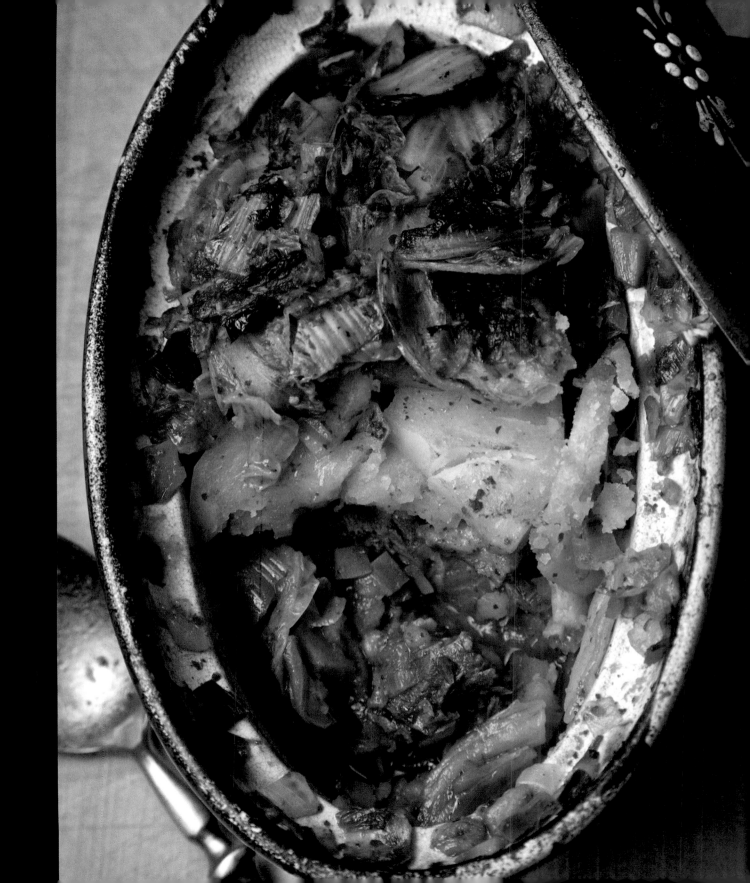

KOREAN BAECKEOFFE

— SERVES 4 —

Baeckeoffe is an old-fashioned Alsatian dish that Jean-Georges grew up eating, mainly for special family occasions. The name means "baker's oven," because traditionally Alsatian women would carry casserole dishes of potatoes, cabbage, and meat to the town baker to cook in the back of his bread oven. In this Korean version, kimchi takes the place of cabbage and the meat is seasoned with *gochugaru* (red pepper powder). The result is a Korean-Alsatian hybrid that perfectly suits our family. The first time Jean-Georges made it I felt like I was falling in love with him all over again.

Preheat the oven to 400°F.

Place half the potatoes in the bottom of a 4-quart baking dish and sprinkle with a little salt. Top with half of the carrots, scallions, garlic, onion, and kimchi. Season the lamb with some salt and the red pepper powder and arrange it on top of the kimchi. Cover the lamb with the remaining potatoes, carrots, scallions, garlic, onion, and kimchi. Pour on just enough wine to cover the ingredients (you probably won't use the entire bottle so it's best to drink the rest). Cover the dish and bake for 2½ hours, checking the liquid level every now and then and adding a splash of wine or water if it's looking very dry, until the vegetables are soft and the lamb is meltingly tender.

Serve hot in soup plates with a nice baguette if you're feeling French or cooked white rice if you're feeling Korean (or both if you're feeling both).

3 large Yukon Gold potatoes (about 8 ounces each), peeled and cut into ¼-inch-thick slices

Coarse salt

2 carrots, coarsely chopped

3 scallions, thinly sliced

4 garlic cloves, thinly sliced

1 small yellow onion, thinly sliced

2 cups coarsely chopped sour kimchi

2 pounds lamb shoulder, cut into 2-inch pieces, large pieces of fat discarded

1 teaspoon gochugaru (red pepper powder)

1 bottle (750ml) white wine, preferably an Alsatian Riesling

A good baguette and/or cooked white rice, for serving

SPICY PORK STIR-FRY

— SERVES 4 —

Jean-Georges spontaneously came up with this dish when we were shooting *Kimchi Chronicles* and it nearly flew off the plate before we had a chance to photograph it. It's insanely good and so quick to make. For a fun variation, lay a piece of foil over your barbecue grate and stir-fry the thinly sliced pork on it. This method of stir-frying on a grill is popular in Korea for picnics and beach meals. Just watch out for the sand. Serve with freshly cooked white rice, which absorbs all of the delicious juices.

2 ½ tablespoons soy sauce

1 tablespoon soju, sake, vodka, or water

2 tablespoons gochujang (red pepper paste)

1 tablespoon gochugaru (red pepper powder)

1 tablespoon sugar

3 scallions, thinly sliced

2 tablespoons finely minced yellow onion

2 garlic cloves, finely minced

1 tablespoon finely minced fresh ginger

1 pound pork loin, thinly sliced

2 tablespoons vegetable oil

1 carrot, cut into strips

4 fresh shiitake mushrooms, stems discarded and caps cut into ⅓-inch-wide slices

1 fresh long red chile pepper, seeded and finely slivered

1 small handful snow peas, halved lengthwise

Cooked white rice, for serving

Whisk together the soy sauce, *soju*, red pepper paste, red pepper powder, sugar, scallions, onion, garlic, and ginger in a large bowl. Add the pork and stir to coat. Cover and let the pork marinate at room temperature for 20 to 30 minutes.

Heat 2 tablespoons of oil in a large nonstick skillet over high heat. Add the pork with all of its marinade. Cook, stirring now and then, until beginning to caramelize, about 2 minutes. Add the carrot, shiitakes, chile pepper, and snap peas and another drop or two of oil if anything is sticking to the pan. Continue to stir and cook until the pork is cooked through and the vegetables are just tender, 3 to 4 minutes.

PORK AND SEAWEED SOUP

— SERVES 4 TO 6 —

Jean-Georges had an inspiring afternoon with Ji-Soon Kim, an amazing cook, teacher, and cookbook author that we nicknamed the "Julia Child of Jeju Island." They shopped for ingredients at the Five Day Market for her special pork stomach, kimchi, and seaweed soup, a dish native to Jeju, an island off the south coast of South Korea. They went back to a traditional *gamasot*-style kitchen, which translates to "big iron cauldron" and is as rustic as can be. The soup—bound with buckwheat flour and tasting of the sea combined with earth—was quickly devoured by Jean-Georges who has since made it at home. He's added a special, decadent twist by topping the soup with crisp slices of the pork belly that he reserved from making the broth—like bacon bits on steroids.

Pork belly stock and reserved pork belly (page 135)

1 large handful of dried wakame or your favorite seaweed

4 cups sour kimchi, chopped, with a bit of its liquid

4 scallions, coarsely chopped

5 garlic cloves, chopped

1 tablespoon vegetable oil

2 teaspoons toasted sesame oil

Freshly ground black pepper

½ cup buckwheat flour

Freshly ground white pepper

1 tablespoon soy sauce

Tender watercress leaves, for garnish

Bring the pork belly stock to a boil in a large stockpot. Meanwhile, soak the seaweed in cold water to cover for 10 minutes. Drain well and coarsely chop.

Add the seaweed, kimchi, scallions, and garlic to the stock. Return the soup to a boil, reduce to a simmer, and cook until the seaweed is completely softened and the soup is infused with flavor, about 20 minutes.

Meanwhile, cut the pork belly (reserved from making the stock) into ½-inch-thick slices. Heat the oil in a large nonstick skillet over medium-high heat. Add the pork belly slices, sprinkle with the sesame oil, and season with black pepper. Cook until browned and crisp on the first side, about 2 minutes. Carefully turn the slices and crisp on the second side, about 1 minute. Set aside.

(recipe continues)

Whisk ½ cup water into the buckwheat flour in a large bowl. It should have the consistency of pancake batter. Stirring constantly, pour the buckwheat mixture into the soup. Season the soup with white pepper. Stir in the soy sauce, adding a bit more if you think the soup needs more salt. Simmer the soup for 5 minutes. Serve each portion with a slice or two of crispy pork. Top with the watercress.

Taxi Food

Like the taxi drivers in New York who know all the small, special hole-in-the-wall places for inexpensive, quick meals (try the Punjabi deli on Houston Street!), Seoul's taxi drivers know the best places for authentic, satisfying Korean food. I was lucky to check out one of their favorite breakfast haunts, which is famous for its soup made with the meaty bones from pigs' backs. Luckily I got there early in the morning because by 11 a.m. it's packed to the brim.

헉스틀라

BEFORE

AFTER

PORK NECK STEW WITH POTATOES AND PERILLA

— SERVES 4 TO 6 —

This is the kind of dish that needs a lot of time and love, but luckily not all that much work. The assertive taste of perilla leaves and seeds is pervasive in this dish, infusing each spoonful of hearty stew with a distinctive aroma and flavor. I make this often on the weekends, letting the broth simmer away for hours.

Place the bones in a large, heavy pot with enough cold water to cover them by 6 inches. Bring to a boil, reduce the heat, and skim off any foam that rises to the surface. Return to a boil and cook for 5 to 6 hours, checking periodically to be sure the water doesn't completely evaporate. The long boil will result in a broth that's cloudy and white and heady.

Stir in the potatoes, onion, *soju*, Umma Paste, *doenjang*, and perilla leaves. Combine the perilla seeds and sesame seeds and grind coarsely in a mortar and pestle and add to the soup. Boil until the potatoes are completely tender but not falling apart, 15 to 20 minutes. Serve the soup bubbling hot, sprinkled with the scallions.

2 pounds pork neck bones

4 medium boiling potatoes, peeled and quartered

1 yellow onion, chopped

1 tablespoon soju, sake, or vodka

Umma Paste (page 23)

3 tablespoons doenjang (soybean paste)

2 dozen perilla leaves, sliced into thin ribbons

2 tablespoons perilla seeds

1 tablespoon roasted sesame seeds

6 scallions, thinly sliced

PORK BELLY STOCK (AND BOILED PORK BELLY)

— MAKES ABOUT 2 QUARTS —

Combine all the ingredients in a large soup pot and add enough cold water just to cover (about 10 cups). Bring to a boil, reduce the heat, and skim off any foam that rises to the surface. Simmer for at least 2 hours and preferably 3. Strain the stock, discarding the vegetables. Reserve the pork belly for Pork and Seaweed Soup (page 130) or *bo ssam* (page 91) or for a decadent chef's snack.

2 pounds pork belly

1 yellow onion, quartered

2-inch piece fresh ginger, sliced into coins

1 bunch scallions, halved crosswise

SIMPLE FRIED CHICKEN WINGS

— SERVES 4 TO 6 —

Once in Seoul I met up with my friends Jennifer and Rachel in Hongdae, the college area. We ate like students—fried chicken and lots of beer. They told me that chicken wings are very popular among Korean women as the collagen is said to be good for the skin. If that's an excuse to eat more, fine by me! I worked hard to perfect this recipe, experimenting with all different ratios of flour and cornstarch, water, and even seltzer. I landed on this simple, light coating of seasoned cornstarch and water that produces the crispiest wings. Fried chicken is often served with pickled white radish, but I also love it with Spicy Marinated Pearl Onions (page 44).

⅓ **cup cornstarch**

Coarse salt and freshly ground black pepper

2 pounds chicken wings, wing tips discarded

Vegetable or safflower oil, for frying

Whisk together the cornstarch and 5 tablespoons water in a large bowl and season aggressively with salt and pepper. Rinse the chicken wings in cool water and pat completely dry with paper towels.

Heat 2 inches of oil in a large heavy pot until hot enough for frying (I like to test the oil by dropping a small piece of torn bread in the oil—it should bubble when you drop it in and begin to get golden brown). Dip the chicken wings in the batter, letting excess batter drip back into the bowl. Working in batches (to avoid crowding), add the chicken wings to the hot oil and cook, turning now and then so that they cook evenly, until nicely browned and cooked through, 11 to 14 minutes. Regulate the oil temperature while you're cooking so that the wings are constantly bubbling and browning but never burning. Drain on a paper towel–lined plate and serve hot.

Fried Chicken

If you love fried chicken as much as I do, which is to say enormously, Korea is an exciting place to visit. Fried-chicken joints, originally imported from the states, have evolved into fully Korean-operated places of skyrocketing popularity, especially in areas with lots of students and lively nightlife. Unlike American fried chicken, which tends toward the salty end of the spectrum, Korean fried chicken is sweet and sticky but no less addictive. Now Korean-style fried chicken (KFC anyone?), full of great flavor and tremendous crunch, has been exported back to the states, where it's become all the rage. At home in New York, I don't need to go far to get a taste of my favorite Korean food.

SPICY AND SWEET FRIED CHICKEN WINGS

— SERVES 4 TO 6 —

Jean-Georges developed the recipe for these crazy delicious chicken wings, which are first marinated with a balanced combination of bright lime and fish sauce with toasty sesame oil and, of course, *gochujang*. They are then dredged in flour and fried and finally tossed with a spicy, sticky, sweet sauce that, while undeniably messy to eat, is purely divine. It's definitely not first-date food, but luckily we're past that. Jean-Georges likes to fry some mild shishito peppers as a garnish and serve with sliced mango.

WINGS AND MARINADE

1 tablespoon sugar

2 tablespoons fresh lime juice

2 tablespoons soy sauce

1 tablespoon fish sauce

1 tablespoon toasted sesame oil

1 tablespoon gochujang
   (red pepper paste)

3 garlic cloves, finely minced

1 tablespoon minced ginger

2 pounds chicken wings

SAUCE

3 tablespoons gochujang
   (red pepper paste)

2 tablespoons rice vinegar

2 tablespoons honey

3 tablespoons gochugaru
   (red pepper powder)

1 tablespoon roasted sesame
   seeds

Vegetable oil, for frying

Flour, for dredging

Coarse salt

To marinate the wings: Whisk the sugar, lime juice, soy sauce, fish sauce, sesame oil, red pepper paste, garlic, and ginger together in a large bowl. Add the chicken wings, stir to coat (gloved hands are the best tool for this job), cover the bowl with plastic wrap, and marinate for 20 minutes at room temperature.

Meanwhile, to make the sauce: Whisk the red pepper paste, vinegar, honey, red pepper powder, and sesame seeds in a large bowl.

Heat 1 inch of oil in a wide deep saucepan until hot enough for frying (I like to test the oil by dropping a small piece of torn bread in the oil—it should bubble when you drop it in and begin to get golden brown). Dredge the wings in flour, shaking off the excess. Working in batches (to avoid crowding), add the wings to the hot oil and cook, turning now and then so that they cook evenly, until browned and crisp and cooked through, about 10 minutes. Transfer the wings to a paper towel–lined plate.

Add the crispy chicken wings to the bowl with the sauce and toss to coat. Pile the wings on a platter and sprinkle with salt.

SAMGYETANG (HEALTHY CHICKEN SOUP)

— SERVES 1 —

Traditionally this dish includes ginseng, but I don't love its medicinal taste so I've left it out. By all means, throw in a small piece if it's your thing. Some variations, like the one that's so famous at Seoul's Tosokchon restaurant, also include ginkgo nuts, chestnuts, pumpkin seeds, and sunflower seeds. If you're really sticking to tradition, also note that *samgyetang* is most popular on the hottest day of summer, a reflection of the belief that hot foods help you regulate your body temperature in hot weather. While this recipe serves only one as per tradition (you get your own small stone pot filled with broth and your very own small chicken), you can easily use a bigger pot, a few more Cornish hens, and more aromatics if you are feeding a crowd.

Rinse the rice in a few changes of cold water and transfer to a bowl. Add cool water to cover and soak for at least 6 hours and up to overnight.

Drain the rice and stir in the garlic and ginger. Stuff the cavity of the Cornish hen with the soaked rice and place in a small stone pot or any small, heavy pot that snugly fits the Cornish hen. Add cold water to cover along with the dried dates. Set the pot over high heat and bring to a boil. Cover and cook at a boil for 1½ hours, checking the water level every 30 minutes or so to ensure that the broth nearly covers the bird. Season the broth to taste with salt (it will take about 1 or 2 teaspoons).

Mix the sesame seeds together in a small bowl with a few grinds of black pepper and a large pinch of salt and set aside. Scatter the soup with scallions and serve the sesame seed mixture alongside. As you eat the soup, use chopsticks to tear off pieces of the succulent Cornish hen that you dip into the sesame-seed mixture as you eat. Enjoy the rice mixed into the soup or in bites on its own. The cooked dates, garlic cloves, and ginger can be eaten, but it's totally okay to leave them at the bottom of the pot too.

½ cup sweet rice

6 garlic cloves, peeled

2-inch piece fresh ginger, peeled

1 Cornish hen

3 dried Korean dates (daechu or jujubes)

Coarse salt

1 teaspoon roasted sesame seeds

Freshly ground black pepper

4 scallions, thinly sliced

EASY BRAISED CHICKEN

I ate a delicious braised chicken dish with vegetables and noodles called *jjimdak* in the city of Andong and another great stir-fry of chicken with vegetables and rice cakes called *dakgalbi* in Chuncheon. Both of these chicken preparations were wonderfully satisfying one-pot meals full of flavor. I combined some of the ingredients and techniques in both of those iconic dishes to come up with the easiest chicken dish in my repertoire, not to mention one of my favorites. In this recipe you just brown a cut-up chicken, add tons of vegetables and a bunch of seasonings, put a lid on it, and in an hour you've got a hearty dinner on the table. This is real Korean home cooking.

One 4-pound chicken

Coarse salt and freshly ground black pepper

2 tablespoons vegetable oil

Umma Paste (page 23)

1 tablespoon soju, sake, vodka, or water

1 tablespoon honey

1 tablespoon roasted sesame seeds

8 small boiling potatoes, peeled

2 medium yellow onions, coarsely chopped

2 carrots, cut into 1-inch pieces

2 bunches scallions, cut into 2-inch pieces

1 fresh green chile pepper, thinly sliced (optional)

1 fresh red chile pepper, thinly sliced (optional)

Cooked white rice, for serving

Cut the chicken into 10 pieces (2 wings, 2 drumsticks, 2 thighs, halve the breasts).

Season the chicken pieces aggressively all over with salt and pepper. Heat the oil in a large, wide heavy pot over high heat. Working in batches if necessary, add the chicken, skin-side down, and brown on both sides, 6 to 7 minutes per side.

Meanwhile, whisk together $^1\!/_2$ cup water, the Umma Paste, *soju*, honey, and sesame seeds. Set the sauce aside.

When all the chicken is browned, add the potatoes, onions, carrots, scallions, and reserved sauce to the pot and stir everything together. Reduce the heat to medium-low, cover, and cook, stirring now and then, until the chicken is cooked through and yielding and the potatoes are tender, 1 hour to 1 hour 15 minutes.

Sprinkle with chiles if you'd like, and serve with rice.

Five

생선과 해산물

FISH AND SHELLFISH

Koreans take their seafood seriously. Surrounded on three sides by water, the South Korean peninsula is bordered by plentiful fishing waters (to the west, there's the Yellow Sea; to the south, the Korea Strait; and to the east, the Sea of Japan, often referred to as the Eastern Sea by Koreans). The country has a major port every hundred miles on its nearly 1,500 miles of coastline.

This fortunate geography and active seafood economy offer kitchens all over the country a terrific variety of high-quality fresh fish and shellfish. It's served raw, fried until irresistibly crisp, boiled into delicious soups and stews, or broiled whole. It's also often dried, a traditional means of preparation. Dried anchovies are the base of many flavorful stocks, and you find dried squid sold nearly everywhere; it's eaten as a snack, usually with a little dish of *gochujang* and mayonnaise—think of it like squid jerky. Salted shrimp are also an important ingredient in Korean cooking, essential for seasoning many types of kimchi and also a key ingredient in *bo ssam* (page 91).

From minimal to sophisticated, Korean cuisine uses the sea's bounty in all sorts of delectable, exciting ways. On Jeju Island, for example, you can enjoy dishes ranging from the absolute simplest—raw sea urchin eaten straight from the ocean—to the more complex, including preparations like Sea Urchin, Mussel, and Seaweed Soup (page 161).

In our kitchen at home, we are often inspired by Korean ingredients and use them to transform some familiar dishes. With the use of sesame oil and red pepper powder, Jean-Georges has successfully Korean-ized tuna tartare and crab fritters, two of his most iconic appetizers—and while both of those dishes are special enough to be served in his restaurants, they're simple enough to prepare at home. And then there's the crown jewel of this chapter: Beer-Battered Fish and Onion Rings with Kimchi Tartar Sauce (page 170). The most flavorful, crisp version of fish-and-chips around, the recipe uses Korean beer and seasonings in the batter and spikes the tartar sauce with kimchi. I say *yes!*

TUNA TARTARE

Jean-Georges has been serving tuna tartare for years—long before it became a fixture on restaurant menus everywhere. This version, which he serves at many of his restaurants, gets a Korean boost from scallions, *gochugaru* (red pepper powder), fresh ginger, and soy sauce. Salmon would work equally well in this recipe. Also note that the recipe makes more dressing than you need for this dish. It keeps covered in the fridge for up to a week and is a delicious accompaniment for anything involving avocado and also makes an excellent marinade for tuna, chicken, or salmon.

Place the tuna in a bowl set over a larger bowl filled with ice (this helps keep it as cold as possible). Toss the tuna with the scallions, 1 tablespoon of the oil, the red pepper powder, and salt.

Combine the remaining ½ cup oil, the ginger, vinegar, honey, and soy sauce in a blender and puree.

Divide the avocado among 4 bowls and evenly distribute the tuna on top. Drizzle 2 tablespoons of the ginger dressing around each portion and top with the radish slices. Drizzle a bit of hot chile oil if you'd like.

½ **pound sushi-grade tuna, cut into thin strips (like noodles)**

2 **scallions, thinly sliced**

1 **tablespoon plus ½ cup extra-virgin olive oil**

Large pinch of gochugaru (red pepper powder)

Large pinch of coarse salt

½ **cup coarsely chopped fresh ginger**

¼ **cup rice vinegar**

¼ **cup honey**

¼ **cup soy sauce**

1 **avocado, thinly sliced**

1 **red radish, thinly sliced**

Hot chile oil, for serving (optional)

SEAFOOD AND SCALLION PAJEON (CRISPY SEAFOOD AND SCALLION PANCAKES)

— MAKES ABOUT 4 LARGE PANCAKES —

These could be called "Don't-Skimp-on-the-Shrimp Pajeon" since they're loaded with what my entrepreneurial husband refers to as "a lot of merchandise." The secret to these pancakes, besides the generous amount of seafood, is the little bit of rice flour which is the key to making them extra crispy. Alternatively, you can leave out the seafood and increase the scallions to make this dish completely vegetarian.

Whisk together the flours and salt in a medium bowl. Whisk in 2 1/4 cups cold water. Fold in the oysters, shrimp, and scallions.

Heat 2 tablespoons of vegetable oil in a large nonstick skillet over medium-high heat. Ladle in a generous cup of the batter (try to get an equal amount of seafood in each pancake) and cook until browned and crisp on the first side, 2 to 4 minutes. Carefully flip the pancake and cook on the second side until browned and crispy, another 2 to 3 minutes. Continue with the remaining batter and more oil as necessary. Serve hot with the Scallion Dipping Sauce.

2 cups unbleached all-purpose flour

1/4 cup rice flour

2 teaspoons coarse salt

8 small oysters, shucked, or 1 container (8 ounces) oysters, drained

1 dozen medium shrimp, peeled, deveined, and halved crosswise

1/2 cup scallion pieces (1 1/2-inch)

Vegetable oil, for frying

Scallion Dipping Sauce (page 27)

LANGOUSTINES WITH CITRUS MAYONNAISE

— SERVES 4 —

When we stayed at the Podo Hotel on Jeju Island, Jean-Georges and his dear friend Magnus took over the kitchen and prepared a meal for the entire crew of *Kimchi Chronicles*. They shopped at the Five Day Market and made a veritable feast including broiled fish with Jean-Georges's Fast, Hot Kimchi (page 42), sautéed local mushrooms and greens, and the most delicious steamed local langoustines that we all peeled at the table and dipped into mayonnaise flavored with *haliabong*, a delicious citrus fruit that grows on the island. At home, tangerines make a fine substitute.

Combine the seaweed and 1 quart of water in a large pot and bring to a boil. Add the langoustines and boil just until bright red, about 5 minutes.

Meanwhile, whisk together the mayonnaise, tangerine zest and juice, and salt. Serve the langoustines immediately with the mayonnaise and a large pile of napkins.

1 large handful fresh seaweed (any kind is fine) or a 4-inch square of dried kelp

2 pounds langoustines (or jumbo shell-on shrimp)

1 cup mayonnaise (homemade if possible)

1 teaspoon grated tangerine zest

1 tablespoon fresh tangerine juice

Pinch of coarse salt

— SERVES 4 —

When Jean-Georges and I visited the AmorePacific green tea gardens in Jeju Island, we were able to witness the entire process of tea making from the soil to the teacup. We learned how each type of tea is grown, harvested, roasted, and packaged and how the ingredients are used to their full potential in the brand's cosmetics (which I swear by). Seeing the care invested in each step was extraordinary; for example, the expert tea pickers never use harsh soap to wash their hands in order to ensure the delicacy and subtleties of each leaf. The plants are 35 years old and apparently only get better as they get older, which reminded Jean-Georges of picking grapes in his native Alsace. When we returned to New York, he prepared two scallop recipes: this one made with raw scallops, and a grilled scallop recipe (page 108). Both celebrate the great flavor combination of sweet shellfish and earthy tea.

8 sea scallops, sliced horizontally into thin discs

Coarse salt

Gochugaru (red pepper powder)

¹/₂ lime

3 tablespoons olive oil

Green tea powder

Divide the scallop slices artfully among 4 plates or 4 clean scallop shells. Sprinkle each serving with a pinch of salt and a pinch of red pepper powder. Evenly squeeze the lime over the scallops and drizzle with the olive oil. Top each serving with a pinch of green tea powder. Let the scallops sit for 5 minutes to marinate before serving.

HAEMUL JEONGOL, AKA JEJU BOUILLABAISSE

Being able to consume ingredients at their source is a bit of an ultimate for chefs. In Jeju Island, Jean-Georges and his friend Magnus went on an exciting adventure with the haenyos (the ladies who dive for sea urchin and abalone). They dove alongside the women—admiring their ability, skill, and lively sense of humor—and then ate sea urchin straight from the ocean. Afterward they had a feast of this mixed seafood stew that was worthy of their well-earned appetites. I've re-created the dish many times at home and it's a real crowd pleaser.

Bring 2 quarts of water to a boil in a wide pot. Add the kimchi, return to a boil, and cook for 5 minutes. Add the onion, radish, Umma Paste, fish sauce, and salt and cook for 10 minutes.

Add the cherrystone clams and cover and cook for 1 minute. Add the lobster, cover, and cook for another minute. Add the scallions, cover, and cook for 1 minute. Scatter the squid, mussels, cockles, shrimp, and watercress over the contents of the pot. Cover and cook until the clams and mussels are open and the shrimp and squid are cooked through, 6 to 8 minutes (discard any clams or mussels that haven't opened). Serve directly from the pot to lucky friends and family.

3 cups coarsely chopped sour kimchi

1 onion, coarsely chopped

4 cups thinly sliced white radish (moo or daikon)

¼ cup Umma Paste (page 23)

2 tablespoons fish sauce

½ teaspoon coarse salt

10 cherrystone clams, scrubbed

1 large lobster, halved lengthwise

6 scallions, cut into 2-inch pieces

6 squid, bodies cut crosswise into 1-inch rings, tentacles left whole

1 dozen mussels, scrubbed

1 dozen cockles, scrubbed

1 dozen shell-on medium shrimp

2 handfuls of watercress

제2파랑도

SEA URCHIN, MUSSEL, AND SEAWEED SOUP

— SERVES 4 TO 6 —

During our visit to Jeju Island, Jean-Georges, Chloe, and I visited with a noted local artist named Mr. Lee. He and his wife took us to their favorite restaurant near their home where we enjoyed great seafood, including a soup made with sea urchin. Back home in New York, Jean-Georges combined that soup with traditional Birthday Seaweed Soup (page 57) to create this sophisticated, totally oceanic soup that would make any occasion a celebration.

Bring 3 quarts of water to a boil in a large soup pot. Place the anchovies and kelp in a metal strainer and submerge in the boiling water. Reduce the heat and simmer for 20 minutes to fully infuse the broth with flavor.

Meanwhile, soak the seaweed in cold water to cover for 10 minutes. Drain well and coarsely chop.

Remove and discard the anchovies and kelp from the broth. Add the chopped seaweed to the broth, cover and boil for 30 minutes.

Meanwhile, heat the oil in a large skillet over medium-high heat. Add the garlic and shallots. Cook, stirring now and then, until a bit softened, about 3 minutes. Add 1 cup water, the soju, white wine, and mussels. Cover the skillet and cook until the mussels open, 5 to 6 minutes. Pour the cooked mussels and their juices on top of the seaweed and its broth in the large soup pot. Scatter the green chiles on top and lay the sea urchin over the mussels. Serve immediately with rice.

20 dried anchovies, heads and innards discarded

6-inch square dried kelp

3 large handfuls of dried wakame or your favorite seaweed

3 tablespoons olive oil

4 garlic cloves, finely minced

2 shallots, finely diced

1/2 cup soju, sake, vodka, or water

1/2 cup dry white wine

2 pounds mussels, scrubbed and debearded

2 teaspoons thinly sliced green chile pepper

1 dozen sea urchin roes

Cooked white rice, for serving

GEJANG (SOY-MARINATED CRABS)

— SERVES 6 —

I went to Pro Ganjang Gejang, one of the most famous crab restaurants in Seoul, to enjoy *gejang*, a famous Korean dish of marinated raw crabs (pictured opposite). The restaurant is run by Ms. Baek-Ja Seo, who is 69 but somehow ageless and has the most amazing passion for her craft and an unbelievable smile. She taught us to mix the roe that was left in the crab shells with rice and a bit of the marinade—really the highlight of the dish. I've adapted this dish for the American kitchen by steaming the crabs first and then marinating them just overnight (as opposed to days on end). The marinade, incidentally, is a delicious seasoned soy sauce that would be equally good with chicken or salmon.

10 garlic cloves, peeled and crushed with the side of a knife

1 coarsely chopped red chile pepper

1 coarsely chopped green chile pepper

2-inch piece fresh ginger, sliced into coins

1 large yellow onion, coarsely chopped

1 cup dried Korean dates (daechu or jujubes), halved

4 cups soy sauce

2 dozen live blue crabs

Cooked white rice, for serving

Combine the garlic, chiles, ginger, onion, jujubes, and soy sauce in a saucepan and bring to a boil over high heat. Reduce the heat to medium and cook for 20 minutes.

Strain the sauce, pressing on the solids to get as much flavor out as possible. Keep the sauce warm while you prepare the crabs.

Meanwhile, steam the crabs in a basket set over boiling water until bright orange, 5 to 10 minutes. When they're just cool enough to handle, flip them over and cut off the flap on the underside, clean out any whiskers and gills, and remove the top shell. Cut them in half to allow more sauce to penetrate the crab. Put the cleaned crabs in a large baking dish or other container that can hold them comfortably and also hold 3 quarts of liquid. Pour the soy sauce mixture over the crabs along with 8 cups of water, being sure to submerge them. Tightly cover the container with its lid or plastic wrap and refrigerate overnight.

Remove the crabs from the marinade (but don't drain them too thoroughly—you want a bit of liquid with each bite) and serve cold with lots of napkins. As you eat the crabs, if you're lucky enough to find any roe or tomalley (the liver), be sure to mix it with some hot white rice for a great treat.

JEAN-GEORGES'S CRAB FRITTERS WITH DIPPING SAUCE

— SERVES 6 —

Jean-Georges put a Korean spin on his crab fritters, one of his most classic and revered dishes, by seasoning them with *gochugaru* and swapping out his usual condiments for a *gochujang*-based dipping sauce. Light and crisp, these fritters should be eaten as soon as they're cooked.

Bring the butter and ½ cup of water to a simmer in a saucepan over medium heat. Add the flour and stir until the dough forms a ball and comes clean from the bottom of the pot. Transfer the dough to a stand mixer and beat with the paddle attachment on medium speed (or alternatively, transfer to a bowl and use a wooden spoon and some muscle). Add the eggs, one at a time, and beat until completely incorporated.

Add the crab and red pepper powder and gently mix together (a gloved hand works very well) just to bind the mixture, being careful not to break up the crab too much.

Whisk together the red pepper paste, vinegar, sesame oil, sugar, and sesame seeds. Set the dipping sauce aside.

Heat ½ inch of oil in a large, deep skillet over medium-high heat. When it's quite hot (I like to test the oil by dropping a small piece of torn bread in the oil—it should bubble when you drop it in and begin to get golden brown), add the crab mixture by tablespoonfuls taking care not to crowd the pan. Cook until browned and crispy on the first side, about 1½ minutes. Carefully flip and cook until browned and crispy on the second side, 1 to 2 minutes. Drain on a paper towel–lined plate.

Serve hot with reserved dipping sauce and sticks of Korean pear.

4 tablespoons (½ stick) unsalted butter

½ cup unbleached all-purpose flour

2 eggs

8 ounces jumbo lump crabmeat

Pinch of gochugaru (red pepper powder)

3 tablespoons gochujang (red pepper paste)

1½ tablespoons rice vinegar

2½ teaspoons toasted sesame oil

1 teaspoon sugar

1 teaspoon roasted sesame seeds

Vegetable oil, for frying

1 Korean (Asian) pear, peeled and cut into ⅓-inch-thick sticks

Fish Market

Jean-Georges had a memorable experience when he visited Noryangjin, Seoul's huge fish market, which could fill several football stadiums. It's a fast-paced market filled with men wearing tall rubber boots, motorcyclists hauling deliveries, women supporting trays of food on their heads, merchandise packed in water-filled bags with fish still swimming inside. Jean-Georges and his friend Magnus went with my friend Diara and marveled at the still-jumping fish, the lively auction, the pristine squid, sea squirts, and other sea creatures. The best part about Noryangjin is that you can buy fish downstairs and bring it to a restaurant upstairs, where it becomes breakfast. Jean-Georges picked out a flounder and an unassuming female fishmonger swiftly cut off its head, then deftly filleted the fish using nothing but a vegetable knife. Jean-Georges watched her intently and tried to hire her on the spot. Needless to say she was happy with her day job. Jean-Georges took the fillets and the bones and the head to a restaurant where the fillets were cut into thin pieces and eaten raw with vinegar-thinned *gochujang*, sliced chile peppers, raw garlic, and perilla leaves. The bones and head were turned into a soul-satisfying soup with vegetables and chile. What a way to start the day!

에스타라

CRUNCHY FRIED SQUID WITH MARMALADE DIPPING SAUCE

— SERVES 4 —

These incredibly crunchy (and therefore incredibly addictive) fried squid make an awesome Korean po' boy sandwich. Spread a crusty roll with mayonnaise and use finely shredded cabbage kimchi instead of lettuce or coleslaw. Pile on the fried squid, get a stack of napkins, and go for it!

1 tablespoon Korean honey citron marmalade or orange marmalade

2 tablespoons soy sauce

1 tablespoon rice vinegar

1 teaspoon gochugaru (red pepper powder)

Pinch of grated fresh ginger

2 cups unbleached all-purpose flour

$1/3$ cup cornstarch

$1/4$ cup panko breadcrumbs

Coarse salt and freshly ground black pepper

1 egg

Vegetable oil, for frying

1 pound squid (cut crosswise into $1/2$-inch rings) or 1 pound medium shrimp (peeled and deveined) or $1/2$ pound each

Whisk together the marmalade, soy sauce, vinegar, red pepper powder, and grated ginger in a small bowl. Set the marmalade dipping sauce aside.

Whisk together 1 cup of the flour, the cornstarch, panko, 1 tablespoon salt, and $1/2$ teaspoon black pepper in a shallow bowl. In a second shallow bowl, beat the egg with a bit of salt and pepper. Place the remaining 1 cup flour in a third shallow bowl.

Heat 2 inches of oil over medium-high heat in a large, heavy pot until very hot (I like to test the oil by dropping a small piece of torn bread in the oil—it should bubble when you drop it in and begin to get golden brown).

Set up the shallow bowls in this order: plain flour, egg, flour-panko mixture. In an assembly-line fashion, dredge the squid and/or shrimp first in the plain flour, then in the egg, and lastly in the panko mixture, shaking the excess off after each step. Working in batches (to avoid crowding the pan), add the seafood to the hot oil and cook until browned and crispy, about 2 minutes. Drain on a paper towel–lined plate.

Serve with the reserved marmalade dipping sauce.

Fry Like a Korean

Koreans have a thing for texture. You'll notice a lot of crunch in Korean cuisine—from the crisp bite of a lettuce leaf wrapped around your favorite barbeque to the edges of savory pancakes like *bindaetteok* (page 67) and *pajeon* (page 151). That said, the crunchiest Korean food comes straight from the fryer. Little places—one of my favorites is Sak Fry, a tiny hole-in-the-wall in Seoul—dot the entire country and make mouthwatering snacks that go way beyond the french fry. I'm especially fond of fried peppers stuffed with ground pork, delicious battered shrimp, and even crispy slices of carrots and sweet potatoes

BEER-BATTERED FISH AND ONION RINGS WITH KIMCHI TARTAR SAUCE

— SERVES 4 —

This is fish-and-chips, Korean style. Make it once and you'll be hooked. I usually make this with Korean beer—Hite and Max are both great brands to look out for. Any kind of beer works well though, as does seltzer.

1½ cups mayonnaise (preferably homemade)

3 scallions, thinly sliced

¾ cup finely chopped kimchi, plus ½ cup kimchi liquid

1 cup unbleached all-purpose flour

½ cup sweet rice powder, plus about 1 cup for dredging the fish

1 tablespoon gochugaru (red pepper powder)

1 tablespoon roasted sesame seeds

2 teaspoons coarse salt

1 egg, beaten

2 tablespoons fish sauce

1½ cups beer or seltzer

Vegetable or canola oil, for frying

2 yellow onions, cut into ½-inch-thick slices and separated into rings

2 red snapper, cod, or sea bass fillets (about 8 ounces each), skinned and cut into 2-inch pieces

Whisk together the mayonnaise, scallions, kimchi, and kimchi liquid. Set the kimchi tartar sauce aside.

Whisk together the all-purpose flour, rice powder, red pepper powder, sesame seeds, and salt in a large bowl. Whisk in the egg, fish sauce, and beer.

Heat 1 inch of oil in a large, deep skillet over medium-high heat (I like to test the oil by dropping a small piece of torn bread in the oil—it should bubble when you drop it in and begin to get golden brown). Dip the onion rings into the beer batter just to coat them and carefully place in the hot oil (the onion rings should sizzle on contact). Let them get browned and crispy on the first side, 1 to 2 minutes. Turn the onion rings and let them get browned and crispy on the second side, another 1 to 2 minutes. Drain on a paper towel–lined plate.

Place 1 cup of rice powder in a shallow bowl. Dredge the fish in the rice powder and then dip into the beer batter. Make sure the oil is still good and hot (reheat if necessary) and fry the fish until browned and crispy, about 2 minutes per side. Drain the fish on a paper towel–lined plate.

Serve the fish with a tall pile of onion rings and the reserved kimchi tartar sauce.

밥 과 국 수

RICE AND NOODLES

Rice and noodles are the ultimate comfort foods in Korean cuisine, reliable stand-bys that are eaten with everything. Since nearly all Korean food is cooked on the stovetop (in fact, ovens are very rare in Korean kitchens), rice and noodles take the place of bread. If you find yourself eating a Korean meal without rice there's probably something off in the world.

While most main dishes like stews and meats are served communally, rice is always a personal affair and each person at any table gets his own small, personal bowl. Rice is also incorporated into dishes, becoming a canvas for dishes like fried rice made delectable with kimchi and also what might be Korea's most famous dish of all, *bibimbap*. Rice comes in different forms in Korean cooking too. In powdered form it's used to thicken seasonings and sauces and also makes *pajeon* (page 151) super crunchy. Toothsome, savory rice cakes go into soups and get tossed with spicy sauces. Sweet rice cakes are decorative and colorful and fill display cases at sweet shops as if they were jewelry.

My Korean mother taught me the best, most foolproof way to make rice. Wash the rice at least three times—really abuse it! The more starch you are able to wash

off, the better your rice will be. Put the washed rice into your rice cooker (can't live without it!) and cover it with water. How much? Here's the secret: Put your rice in the rice cooker and place the tip of your index finger on the rice so that you're pointing straight down. Add enough water to come up to the first knuckle on your finger. It works every time.

Noodles inspire some of my most favorite dishes in the Korean repertoire. Like an Italian eating spaghetti, I feel most at home with a bowl of *jajangmyeon* in front on me or a large serving of soup with thick noodles and a heady broth. Noodles, in other words, equal satisfaction. Noodles also equal variety—some are made of wheat, some of sweet potato, others of buckwheat; some noodles are eaten in cold soups, others in hot soups, some in stir-fries. Many are rolled and cut by machine, others cut by hand (known as *kalguksu*).

The recipes in this chapter are close to my heart—it s the food I crave and the food I make most often.

BIBIMBAP (RICE BOWL)

— SERVES 1 GENEROUSLY —

Made completely from scratch, *bibimbap* can seem like a lot of work, but it's much less labor-intensive if you think of it as a vehicle for reinventing leftovers. *Bibimbap* is actually much like a chopped salad—a dish that magically makes use of all the odds and ends in your vegetable bin—in the form of a rice bowl. For *dolsot bibimbap*, a variation that has a signature (and addictive) crust on the bottom, it's traditionally made in a Korean stone pot, but you can certainly use a cast iron pan instead. Additionally, you can enjoy *bibimbap* as a cold dish made with room-temperature rice and toppings, all bound together with the *bibimbap* sauce. Treat the ingredients listed below as a recommendation—the world is your rice bowl.

Whisk together the red pepper paste, 1 tablespoon of the sesame oil, the vinegar, and sesame seeds in a small bowl. Set the sauce aside until serving (it will keep, covered in the fridge for 1 week).

Cover the seaweed with cold water and let it sit for at least 10 minutes.

Meanwhile, bring 4 cups of water to a boil in a small saucepan. Place the shiitakes in a small heatproof bowl, ladle ½ cup of the boiling water over them, and set aside for 10 minutes to soften. Add the spinach to the boiling water and cook until bright green and completely wilted, not more than 1 minute. Drain the spinach and rinse with cold water to stop it from cooking any further. Squeeze the spinach to remove as much of the water as possible and set aside. Drain the shiitakes, slice off and discard the stems, thinly slice the caps and set aside.

Heat 1 tablespoon of the sesame oil in a small nonstick skillet over medium heat. Add the zucchini and a pinch of salt and cook, stirring now and then, until the zucchini is just tender, 3 to 4 minutes. Set the zuchinni aside.

(recipe continues)

2 tablespoons gochujang (red pepper paste)

5 tablespoons toasted sesame oil

2 teaspoons rice vinegar

1 teaspoon roasted sesame seeds

1 handful dried seaweed, any kind you prefer

2 dried shiitake mushrooms

2 large handfuls of baby spinach leaves

½ small zucchini, cut into long matchsticks

Coarse salt

Small handful of fresh bean sprouts

1½ cups cooked rice

1 egg

¼ cup leftover bulgogi (page 120)

¼ cup Seasoned Radish (page 197)

Heat another tablespoon of sesame oil in the same skillet, add the bean sprouts and a pinch of salt, and cook, stirring now and then, until the bean sprouts are lightly browned and a bit limp, about 3 minutes. Set the bean sprouts aside.

Drain the seaweed and roughly chop it. Heat another tablespoon of sesame oil in the same skillet, add the seaweed, and cook until it wilts, stirring now and then, about 4 to 5 minutes. Set the seaweed aside.

Meanwhile, heat a stone pot or a small cast iron skillet over high heat for at least 5 minutes. Pack the rice into the hot pot or skillet and leave it over the flame for 2 minutes. Carefully take it off the heat, cover, and let sit for 5 minutes (this will help it develop its signature crust).

While the rice is resting, heat the remaining 1 tablespoon sesame oil in the same small nonstick skillet. Add the egg and cook until it's cooked to your preference (I like mine quite runny). Uncover the rice and place the fried egg on top and then arrange the seaweed, shiitakes, spinach, zucchini, bean sprouts, *bulgogi*, and Seasoned Radish in small piles around the egg. Eat by adding as much of the reserved sauce as you'd like and mixing everything together (*bibimbap* translates to "mixed rice"!).

Roya Court Cuisine

Royal court cuisine originated during the Joseon Dynasty (1392–1910). Opulent menus were created to highlight the specialties of Korea's different regions. Dishes can include familiar foods like *bibimbap*, but also unusual and special things like *sinseollo* (similar to a Chinese hot pot) and *gujeolpan*, an elaborate assortment of nine ingredients served with pancakes to roll them in. Royal court meals always end with lots of sweet rice cake treats (*tteok*) made with intricate designs and colors. Whatever wasn't consumed by royalty was passed down to the next class, and so on. In turn foods that were originally exclusive became popular with the masses.

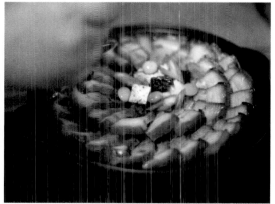

엑스트라

GIMBAP (RICE AND FILLINGS WRAPPED WITH SEAWEED)

— MAKES 4 ROLLS —

Essentially Korean sushi, *gimbap* is rolls of rice and other fillings wrapped in seaweed and cut into bite-size pieces. It's a cheap snack, a quick lunch, and most often served after school and for picnics. Like *bibimbap*, it's a great vehicle for leftovers. It almost always includes carrot, spinach, and egg; other fillings range from kimchi with canned tuna to leftover *bulgogi* with pickled daikon—I've even seen leftover fried chicken with mayonnaise and kimchi used as a filling. The following is my personal favorite, but when I make it with Chloe we always include kimchi and American cheese (the cheese makes it happen).

Lay one piece of seaweed on a sushi rolling mat or on a large piece of plastic wrap. Mix the rice with the salt, sugar, and vinegar and spread one-quarter of it in a thin layer over the entire piece of seaweed. Arrange one-quarter of the egg, spinach, carrot, and pickled daikon, and 1 slice each of American cheese and ham evenly over the rice.

Use the mat to help you roll the *gimbap* into a tight cylinder. Repeat the process with the remaining ingredients to make 3 more rolls. Use a sharp knife to slice the rolls in sushilike pieces, dipping the blade in water before each cut.

Note: Follow the instructions in the recipe for *tangpyeongchae* (page 72) for making a thin egg omelet.

- **4 sheets toasted gim or nori seaweed**
- **2 cups warm cooked short-grain white rice**
- **1/2 teaspoon coarse salt**
- **1/2 teaspoon sugar**
- **4 teaspoons rice vinegar**
- **1 thin egg omelet (see Note), sliced into ribbons**
- **1/2 cup sautéed spinach (page 45)**
- **1 large carrot, cut into matchsticks**
- **A few strips pickled daikon**
- **4 slices American cheese**
- **4 slices deli ham**

KIMCHI FRIED RICE

This recipe couldn't be simpler. It's one of the best ways to use leftover rice—something I often seem to have a lot of—and its success is actually based on the dryness of day-old rice, which browns and crisps much better than fresh, soft rice. One of my most guilty, happiest pleasures is to make this late at night (usually after a lot of karaoke) and eat it with cheese (slices of American melted into it, if you must know . . .).

2 tablespoons toasted sesame oil

1½ cups finely chopped onions

Pinch of coarse salt

2 cups sour kimchi, coarsely chopped, plus ¼ cup kimchi liquid

4 cups day-old cooked rice, at room temperature

Heat the sesame oil in a large nonstick skillet over medium-high heat. Add the onions and salt. Cook, stirring now and then, until beginning to soften and brown, about 3 minutes. Add the kimchi and cook for 1 minute to combine nicely with the onion. Add the rice and stir thoroughly to combine. Cook until the rice is warmed through and beginning to brown, about 5 minutes. Serve hot.

JEAN-GEORGES'S GINGER FRIED RICE

— SERVES 4 —

Mark Bittman, noted cookbook author and food journalist, has worked with, and been friends with, Jean-Georges for years. He published a version of this recipe in the *New York Times* not too long ago and it's become quite popular. The combination of simple ingredients and techniques smartly brought together to make a sum that's more ethereal than its parts is sort of my husband's stamp—each of his dishes is really an assembly of simple steps. In this version, Jean-Georges uses Korean *gochugaru* (red pepper powder) to add color and spice. The runny, rich egg yolk against the spicy, slightly crispy rice is just heaven.

Heat 4 tablespoons of the vegetable oil in a small nonstick skillet over high heat. Add 1 tablespoon each of the garlic and ginger and cook until golden brown and crisp, 1 to 2 minutes. With a slotted spoon, transfer the garlic and ginger to a paper towel–lined plate. Sprinkle with a pinch of salt and set aside.

Heat 3 tablespoons of the vegetable oil in a large skillet over medium heat. Add the remaining ginger and garlic and cook for about 30 seconds to allow the flavors to bloom. Add the leeks and cook until beginning to soften, about 2 minute. Add the rice and cook, stirring often, until warmed through and beginning to brown, about 5 minutes. Season with salt and about ½ teaspoon red pepper powder.

Heat the remaining 1 tablespoon vegetable oil in a nonstick skillet. Break the eggs into the pan and fry until cooked to your preference. Sprinkle each egg with a pinch of red pepper powder.

Transfer the rice to 4 individual dishes and top with the fried eggs. Sprinkle with the reserved fried garlic and ginger, then drizzle each egg with the sesame oil and soy sauce. Serve hot.

8 tablespoons vegetable oil
3 tablespoons minced garlic
3 tablespoons minced fresh ginger
Coarse salt
2 cups sliced leeks
4 cups day-old cooked rice, at room temperature
Gochugaru (red pepper powder)
4 large eggs
2 teaspoons toasted sesame oil
2 teaspoons soy sauce

JUK WITH WILD MUSHROOMS

— SERVES 4 —

Jean-Georges put his spin on *juk*, Korean rice porridge that's similar to Chinese congee, to create a savory, hearty dish that's often eaten for breakfast. It's the best way to start a long day.

1 cup short-grain rice

2 tablespoons toasted sesame oil, plus more for serving

2 garlic cloves, finely minced

2 scallions, thinly sliced

3 cups coarsely chopped fresh wild mushrooms (see Note)

Small handful of mint or basil leaves and baby chives (or extra chopped scallions) for garnish

2 teaspoons soy sauce

Place the rice in a bowl and add cold water to cover by 1 inch. Let soak for at least 1 hour. Drain the rice and place in a soup pot with 10 cups of water. Bring to a boil, reduce to a simmer, cover, and cook, stirring now and then, until it forms a nice soft porridge, about 45 minutes.

Meanwhile, heat the 2 tablespoons sesame oil in a large nonstick skillet over medium-high heat. Add the garlic and scallions and cook for 30 seconds just to get a wonderful fragrance in the air. Add the mushrooms and cook, stirring now and then, until they're wilted, about 4 minutes.

Ladle the porridge into 4 big bowls. Spoon the mushrooms evenly over each portion. Garnish with micro perilla leaves and baby chives (or scallions) and drizzle each serving with a little sesame oil and the soy sauce.

Note: Jean-Georges uses a mix of hen-of-the-woods, shiitakes, chanterelles, blue foot, black trumpets, or king oyster, but use whatever you can find.

KALGUKSU

This broth converts even the most adamant anchovy haters out there. Instead of tasting fishy or funky as some might expect, this soup has only a remarkable depth of flavor that's completely satisfying.

4 garlic cloves, minced

2 teaspoons dashida or fish sauce

20 dried anchovies, heads and innards discarded

6-inch square dried kelp

6 scallions, cut into 1-inch pieces

1 pound kalguksu noodles or udon noodles

2 eggs, beaten

4 sheets toasted gim or nori seaweed

Combine the garlic, *dashida,* and 3 quarts of water in a large heavy pot. Place the anchovies and kelp in a metal sieve and lower it into the water. Bring to a rolling boil over high heat and continue to boil for 15 minutes. Remove the sieve with the anchovies and kelp.

Add the scallions and noodles and cook until the noodles are just soft when you bite into one (test after 5 minutes). Just before serving, stir the soup with a large spoon and pour in the eggs while stirring. They will cook instantly and break into small, feathery bits. Ladle the soup and noodles into bowls and crumble a sheet of seaweed over each serving.

Slurp Noodles

Not only is it not considered rude to slurp your noodles in Korea, it is downright encouraged. Slurping is both emotional and functional—it shows respect for the person who prepared the noodles (i.e., "these are so delicious, I can't eat them fast enough!") and it also cools the noodles down as you eat them. My daughter, Chloe, is great at slurping her noodles, gracefully eating long noodles one at a time. Whatever your approach, don't be shy.

엑스트라

RICE CAKE SOUP WITH BRISKET

— SERVES 4 —

It's a tradition in Korea to start the New Year with a bowl of this satisfying soup. The broth works equally well with noodles instead of sliced rice cakes. When I make the noodle variation, I like to add a thinly sliced zucchini to the soup right when the noodles go in. For that version I also usually omit the egg, as the noodles thoroughly thicken the broth and the egg seems a bit like overkill. But, as always, to each his own!

Combine the rice cakes with cold water to cover by 1 inch in a bowl and soak for 1 hour. Drain.

Heat the sesame oil in a large heavy soup pot over medium-high heat. Add the beef and a pinch of salt and cook, stirring now and then, until just browned on all sides, about 5 minutes. Add cold water to cover, cover the pot, increase the heat to high, and cook for 20 minutes at a low boil, skimming any foam that rises to the surface.

Add the *dashida,* drained rice cakes, garlic, and a large pinch of salt. Cook uncovered until when you taste a rice cake you can easily bite through and it isn't opaque in the center (think of it like pasta), about 8 minutes. Add the scallions and cook for 1 minute.

Stir the soup with a large spoon and pour in the eggs while stirring. They will cook instantly and break into small, feathery bits. Ladle the soup and sliced rice cakes into bowls and crumble a piece of seaweed over each serving.

1½ **pounds sliced rice cakes (labeled as tteokguk or dduckguk)**

2 **tablespoons toasted sesame oil**

½ **pound beef brisket, cut across the grain into ¼-inch-thick slices**

Coarse salt

2 **teaspoons dashida or fish sauce**

4 **garlic cloves, minced**

6 **scallions, cut into 2-inch pieces**

2 **eggs, beaten**

4 **sheets toasted gim or nori seaweed**

JAPCHAE (GLASS NOODLE AND VEGETABLE STIR-FRY)

— SERVES 4 —

Japchae is a simple dish of cooked noodles mixed with stir-fried vegetables, all tossed together with a garlicky, sweet soy sauce–based sauce. It's versatile, everyone loves it, and it can be made ahead of time and served at room temperature. Think of it as Korean pasta salad! I often make it just with the traditional mushrooms, onion, bell peppers, carrots, and spinach, but this full-bore version adds Jean-Georges's combination of spring vegetables, which includes asparagus and fresh fava beans. Use whatever vegetables you and your family most enjoy.

Boil the noodles according to package directions. Drain and drizzle with a little sesame oil and set aside.

Whisk together the soy sauce, honey, sesame seeds, and half the garlic in a small bowl. Set the sesame-garlic sauce aside.

Heat 1½ tablespoons each of sesame oil and olive oil in a large wok over high heat. Add the mushrooms, onion, and half the remaining garlic and cook, stirring constantly, until browned and softened, about 4 minutes. Transfer the mushroom mixture to a plate and drizzle with a bit of sesame oil.

Add another 1½ tablespoons each of sesame oil and olive oil to the wok and add the bell peppers and carrot. Cook, stirring constantly, until beginning to soften, about 2 minutes. Add the asparagus, snap peas, fava beans, and green beans and cook until all the vegetables are just barely cooked through, about 2 minutes.

Add the reserved sesame-garlic sauce, the noodles, mushrooms, and pea shoots or spinach and stir just until the greens wilt, about 30 seconds. Serve hot or at room temperature.

Note: You can substitute ½ cup fresh fava beans that have been blanched and peeled; you'll need ½ pound fava bean pods to get ½ cup beans.

1 pound japchae noodles or cellophane noodles

3 tablespoons toasted sesame oil, plus extra for drizzling

½ cup soy sauce

1 tablespoon honey

1 tablespoon roasted sesame seeds

4 large garlic cloves, minced

3 tablespoons olive oil

1½ cups sliced mushrooms

1 small onion, finely diced

3 bell peppers, preferably red, yellow, and orange, slivered

1 large carrot, cut into strips

½ pound thin asparagus, halved lengthwise

1 cup snow peas, halved lengthwise

½ cup thawed frozen peeled fava beans (see Note)

1 small handful thin green beans or haricots verts

3 cups baby spinach leaves

JAJANGMYEON (NOODLES WITH BLACK BEAN SAUCE)

— SERVES 4 —

Like pizza for New Yorkers, *jajangmyeon* is an imported dish (the black bean paste is a Chinese ingredient) that's become part of the Korean identity—it's eaten everywhere, especially late at night and especially as takeout. When I first returned to Korea as a grown-up, the taste brought back a flood of memories. Now I make it at home or eat it in the food court at H Mart, a chain of Korean groceries with a huge store in New Jersey. A word of caution though: Don't get *jajangmyeon* on your clothes as it won't come out.

2 medium boiling potatoes, peeled and cut into ¹/₂-inch cubes

1 zucchini, cut into ¹/₂-inch cubes

1 pound fresh jajangmyeon noodles or fresh Chinese egg noodles

1 tablespoon vegetable oil

1 pound lean pork belly, cut into ¹/₂-inch cubes

Coarse salt and freshly ground black pepper

1 medium onion, coarsely diced

¹/₃ cup black bean paste

1 small Korean cucumber (or ¹/₂ hothouse cucumber, seeded), cut into matchsticks

Gochugaru (red pepper powder)

Bring a pot of salted water to a boil and cook the potatoes until just easily pierced with a knife, being careful not to overcook them, about 10 minutes. Add the zucchini and cook for 1 minute. With a slotted spoon, transfer the vegetables to a sieve or colander and rinse with cold water to stop the cooking.

Add the noodles to the boiling water and cook according to the package directions. Drain and set aside. Meanwhile, heat the oil in a large nonstick skillet over high heat. Add the pork belly, season with salt and pepper, and cook, stirring now and then, until browned and crispy and all the fat is rendered, about 7 minutes. Remove the pork with a slotted spoon to a paper towel–lined plate and discard all but 2 tablespoons of the fat from the skillet.

Add the onion to the skillet and cook until beginning to soften and brown around the edges, about 2 minutes. Add the potatoes and zucchini, a pinch of salt, ¹/₂ teaspoon black pepper, the black bean paste, ³/₄ cup water, and the reserved cooked pork and stir to combine. Bring to a boil, reduce the heat to a simmer, cover, and cook for 10 minutes.

Divide the cooked noodles evenly among 4 serving bowls and evenly ladle the black bean sauce over the noodles. Garnish each bowl with the cucumber and a pinch of red pepper powder.

DONGCHIMI MAEMIL GUKSU (BUCKWHEAT NOODLES WITH COLD WATER KIMCHI BROTH)

— SERVES 1 —

The recipes for the noodles, sauce, and kimchi from Silo Am restaurant are quite secret, but I think the following recipe is just about as close as you can get.

To make the Seasoned Radish: Combine the radish, salt, sugar, vinegar, red pepper paste, and red pepper powder in a small bowl and set aside.

Meanwhile, to make the sauce: Whisk together the sesame oil, garlic, scallions, and remaining 2 tablespoons rice vinegar and 3 tablespoons red pepper paste in another small bowl. Set the garlic-scallion sauce aside.

Bring a pot of water to a boil and cook the noodles according to the package directions. Drain and rinse under cold water. With your hand, coil the noodles directly into your serving bowl. Drizzle over the remaining 2 teaspoons sesame oil and then top with the reserved garlic-scallion sauce, the radish mixture, cucumber, sesame seeds, and seaweed. Add the kimchi and ladle the kimchi liquid over everything.

SEASONED RADISH

1/2 cup large white radish (moo or daikon) matchsticks

Pinch of coarse salt

Pinch of sugar

1 tablespoon rice vinegar

1 tablespoon gochujang (red pepper paste)

1 tablespoon gochugaru (red pepper powder)

3 teaspoons toasted sesame oil

2 garlic cloves, finely minced

3 scallions, thinly sliced

2 tablespoons rice vinegar

3 tablespoons gochujang (red pepper paste)

4 ounces buckwheat noodles

1/2 cucumber, cut into strips

1 teaspoon roasted sesame seeds

1 tablespoon finely shredded toasted gim or nori seaweed

1/2 cup water kimchi (page 41), plus 1 1/2 cups ice cold kimchi liquid

Buckwheat Noodles

The without-a-doubt best buckwheat noodles are served at Silo Am restaurant just outside of the city of Sokcho in northern South Korea, the area where most of my Korean family lives. It's the kind of restaurant that you'd never find unless someone who was clued in told you about it. How lucky were we when we were shooting *Kimchi Chronicles*! Not only did the great tip get us there in the first place, but we returned over and over. It's been run for over 30 years by the same family. Kim, the founder, still works at the restaurant every day alongside her children and grandchildren. Their dedication pays off—their noodles, homemade from buckwheat that they farm and grind themselves, are exemplary and their water kimchi tastes bright and clean.

OI-NENGGUK (BUCKWHEAT NOODLES WITH COLD CUCUMBER SOUP)

— SERVES 2 —

This is great as a summer lunch. It's quick to prepare and very good for digestion. I always serve this with extra vinegar alongside in case anyone wants a little bit more tang.

Bring a pot of water to a boil and cook the noodles according to the package directions. Drain and rinse under cold water. With your hand, coil the noodles directly into 2 serving bowls.

Combine the water, vinegar, soy sauce, red pepper powder, *dashida*, and sesame seeds in a large bowl. Taste for seasoning, adding extra soy sauce or vinegar if you'd like. Place half of the cucumber and scallions over each portion of noodles and evenly divide the cold soup over each serving.

8 ounces buckwheat noodles

2 cups ice cold water

3 tablespoons rice vinegar

2 tablespoons soy sauce

1 teaspoon gochugaru (red pepper powder)

1 teaspoon dashida or fish sauce

1 teaspoon roasted sesame seeds

2 Korean cucumbers (or 1 hothouse cucumber, seeded), cut into thin 2-inch-long sticks

2 scallions, thinly sliced

NAENGMYEON (NOODLES WITH COLD BEEF BROTH)

— SERVES 4 —

Naengmyeon is a very traditional noodle soup that is served icy cold. Following the Korean belief that you should eat cold food in cold weather and hot food in hot weather, *naengmyeon* is supposed to be eaten in frigid temperatures; but it's become popular as a refreshing dish for the summer months as well.

BEEF BROTH

1 pound beef brisket

6 scallions, halved crosswise

2-inch piece fresh ginger, sliced into coins

2 garlic cloves, peeled

1 cup white radish (moo or daikon) matchsticks

1 teaspoon coarse salt

1 teaspoon sugar

3 tablespoons rice vinegar, plus more for serving

1 pound naengmyeon noodles or buckwheat soba noodles

1 cup Korean (Asian) pear matchsticks

1 cup cucumber matchsticks

4 hard-boiled eggs, quartered

Korean hot mustard, for serving

Place the brisket in a large pot and cover with 3 quarts of cold water. Bring to a boil over high heat and skim off any foam that rises to the top. Add the scallions, ginger, and garlic and boil for 2 hours, adding more water if necessary to keep the meat barely covered. Strain the broth, discard the cooked vegetables, and reserve the meat separately. Refrigerate the broth until ice cold, at least 6 hours.

Remove and discard the hardened fat from the broth. Thinly slice the brisket.

Meanwhile, combine the radish with the salt, sugar, and 3 tablespoons vinegar in a small bowl and let sit for at least 10 minutes.

Bring a large pot of water to a boil and cook the noodles according to the package directions. Drain and rinse under cold water. Divide the cold noodles among 4 deep soup bowls.

Evenly ladle the cold beef broth over the noodles. Top each portion with the marinated radish, pear, cucumber, egg, and sliced brisket. Serve with the hot mustard and additional vinegar on the side for guests to stir into their soup if they'd like.

칵테일, 안주 및 해장방법

COCKTAILS, ANJU, AND HANGOVER CURES

A s in many cultures, Koreans tend to gather over drinks. Lots of them. And, just like eating in Korea, drinking has its own set of rituals.

The best part about getting a drink in Korea is that it never arrives without something to eat. At an American bar if you're lucky you might get a little bowl of peanuts or pretzels. In Korea, a simple beer will often come with an array of small dishes, and your drinking companion will likely order a variety of *anju*, the name for food that accompanies drinks. Yes, the food that accompanies drinks gets its own name.

One of the most fun ways to experience drinking culture in Korea is in a tent. The tents are almost all run by women who set up them up each day and break them down every evening (or rather, set them up every night and take them down every morning). They're often located on tucked-away sidewalks, and people get together there for a beer or a shallow bowl of *makgeolli* (a fermented rice beverage), perhaps a shot or two or seven of *soju*. The women also set up small camping stoves or grills and make addictive *anju* like skewers of chicken gizzards or whole garlic cloves sprinkled with salt. My favorite *anju* of all time might actually be the easiest one to prepare: dried squid (which has the texture of beef jerky and tastes like the ocean) that you eat with *gochujang* and mayonnaise. It's a bit like the Korean version of the

classic Spanish tapas, *patatas bravas*, a dish of fried potatoes with garlicky aioli and spicy tomato sauce.

Koreans, being expert drinkers, are very knowledgeable about curing hangovers. In fact, certain dishes are eaten before bed after a long night of drinking to prevent hangovers the following day. On page 219 you'll find my recipe for *budae jjigae*, a stew that will not only prevent a hangover but will also keep you full for about a week. The name means "army stew" and it's packed with ingredients once provided to Koreans by the American army, including sliced hot dogs and diced Spam. It sounds crazy, but it's also one of my ultimate comfort foods and a great example of the resourcefulness of Korean cooks.

You'll also find my go-to cocktails in this chapter, all simple to prepare and fun to drink. The biggest hit might be the Ginger Georgie, cheekily named after my husband, who ingeniously decided to mix ginger syrup (the same syrup he uses for the ginger margaritas at some of his restaurants) with *makgeolli*. And don't overlook the Kimchi Mary (page 211), a Bloody Mary that substitutes kimchi for horseradish, fish sauce for Worcestershire sauce, and *soju* for vodka. Try them all, experiment with your own favorite ingredients and, as always, *gunbae* (cheers)!

Pour a Drink

Pouring a drink in Korea is not a mindless task. In a culture that pays incredible respect to age and reveres its older generations, pouring a drink is an opportunity to show consideration. If you are the youngest one at the table, it's customary to pour for anyone older than you. But if someone older pours you a drink, be sure to hold your glass with both hands to indicate respect and appreciation. By the same token, when someone younger than you pours you a drink or refills your glass, it's fine to hold your glass with just one hand.

DIRTY CUCUMBER KIMCHI MARTINI

— MAKES 1 DRINK —

A classic martini is made with gin and dry vermouth, garnished with a few olives. Swap the olives for another salty, pungent ingredient—kimchi, of course—and substitute a bit of the kimchi liquid for vermouth and you've got yourself a Korean cocktail worthy of James Bond. Cucumber kimchi is a great choice for this cocktail since cucumber and gin are a classic match (although vodka works equally well if you are not a gin lover).

Pour the vodka and kimchi liquid into a cocktail shaker with plenty of ice. Shake for longer than you think you should to be sure it's really, really cold. Put the cucumber kimchi into a martini glass and strain the vodka mixture over it.

2 ounces (¼ cup) gin or vodka

½ ounce (1 tablespoon) cucumber kimchi liquid

Ice

1 bite-size piece cucumber kimchi

KOR ROYALE

A Kir Royale is a traditional French cocktail made with a simple combination of crème de cassis (blackcurrant liqueur) and champagne. Using Korean raspberry wine, which has the same consistency and sweetness of cassis, takes this drink from West to East.

2 tablespoons Korean
raspberry wine
Champagne
Fresh raspberries, for garnish

Fill a champagne flute one-third full with Korean raspberry wine, top off with champagne, and float a couple of raspberries on top.

HALLABONG MARGARITA

— MAKES 4 DRINKS —

This drink takes its vibrant color and deliciously sweet and tart flavor from Korean *hallabong* juice (see page 15). The addition of gochugaru (red pepper powder) on the rim not only looks colorful and festive, but also gives the drink a subtle kick.

¼ cup coarse salt
1 teaspoon gochugaru (red
pepper powder)
1 lime, halved
Ice
2 cups hallabong juice (or
tangerine or orange juice)
6 ounces good-quality silver
tequila
3 tablespoons agave nectar

Mix the salt and gochugaru together in a small dish. Cut one of the lime halves into two wedges and use the cut surfaces to moisten the rims of 4 highball glasses. Dip the glasses into the salt mixture to coat. Fill each glass with ice.

Juice the lime wedges and remaining lime half into a pitcher and add the *hallabong* juice, tequila, and agave. Stir to combine and divide among the 4 prepared glasses.

KIMCHI MARY

The Korean answer to a traditional Bloody Mary. If you want to really set it over the top Korean-style, rub the rim of each glass with a piece of lime and dust it with coarse *gochugaru*.

Mix together the tomato juice, kimchi liquid, fish sauce, chopped kimchi (if using), and lime juice.

Fill 4 tall glasses with ice, add ¼ cup *soju* to each, and top off with the tomato mixture (don't blend; leave the layers separate). Garnish with a pinch of red pepper powder, a celery stick, and a cucumber slice. Let your guests use the veggie sticks to stir everything together.

4 cups tomato juice

⅓ cup spicy, sour kimchi liquid

2 teaspoons fish sauce

⅔ cup finely chopped sour kimchi (optional)

Juice of 1½ limes

Ice

1 cup soju

Gochugaru (red pepper powder)

4 celery sticks

4 long slices cucumber

GINGER GEORGIE

Jean-Georges created this drink by combining *makgeolli*, a Korean rice ale that he came to adore during our visit to Korea, with the ginger syrup that goes into the ginger margaritas at many of his restaurants. It's worth making a big batch of this syrup as it keeps well in the fridge and elevates any drink from typical to memorable.

1 cup sugar
1 cup coarsely chopped fresh ginger
1 cup fresh lime juice
Ice
1 quart makgeolli
1 lime, sliced

Combine the sugar, ginger, and lime juice in a small saucepan. Bring to a boil over high heat and cook just until the sugar is dissolved. Let the syrup cool. Strain and refrigerate until needed.

For each drink, fill a highball glass with ice. Fill the glass three-quarters full with *makgeolli* and add ginger syrup to taste. Stir to combine and garnish with a slice of lime.

J-G-DO

Jean-Georges was inspired to create this cocktail after we visited the green tea fields on Jeju Island. Since it's often called Jeju-do (pronounced "jae-ju-doe"), we came up with the cheeky name "J-G-Do." If you want to make a festive nonalcoholic drink, note that this syrup would mix well with soda water.

¼ cup green tea powder
¼ cup honey
1 cup soju
Ice
4 perilla leaves

Whisk together the green tea powder and honey with ¼ cup water. Fill 4 highball glasses with ice. Evenly distribute the green tea syrup among the 4 glasses and top off with *soju*. Stir each cocktail to blend, tuck a perilla leaf into each, and serve immediately.

SOJU GREYHOUND

— MAKES 1 DRINK —

This refreshing drink is the Korean equivalent of a Salty Dog (gin and grapefruit juice served in a salt-rimmed glass) or a Greyhound (vodka and grapefruit juice). The raspberries not only make the drink awfully pretty, they also become a delicious *soju*-saturated treat.

Fill a highball glass with ice. Squeeze the grapefruit and pour the juice over the ice and top off with *soju*. Stir together, float the raspberries on top, and enjoy.

Ice
1 pink grapefruit
2 ounces ($\frac{1}{4}$ cup) soju
2 or 3 raspberries

SOJU MOJITO

— MAKES 1 DRINK —

Substituting *soju* for rum brings this classic Cuban cocktail into delicious Korean territory. The addition of the perilla leaf also helps make it more distinctly Korean, but if you can't find perilla, surely the drink won't suffer too much.

Muddle the mint, perilla leaf, and sugar together in the bottom of a highball glass. Add the *soju* and lime juice and stir to combine. Fill the glass with ice and top off with the soda water.

6 mint leaves
1 fresh perilla leaf, torn up
1 tablespoon sugar
$1\frac{1}{2}$ ounces soju
Juice of $\frac{1}{2}$ lime
Ice
$\frac{1}{2}$ cup soda water

DUBU KIMCHI (TOFU WITH KIMCHI AND PORK)

— SERVES 4 —

Dubu kimchi is a very traditional Korean *anju*, a flavorful dish that goes nicely with drinks (I almost always order it while my friends and family are out at karaoke!). The combination of subtle tofu with the spice of kimchi and the richness of pork is a well-balanced, delicious combination, not to mention packed with protein. It's often made with thin strips of pork belly, but I like to use ground pork as it's a bit easier to cook. If you'd like a real twist, skip the tofu, substitute a pound of ground pork for the diced pork belly, and serve the mixture on small hamburger buns for Korean Sloppy Joes!

2 tablespoons toasted sesame oil

$1/4$ cup finely diced onion

2 garlic cloves, minced

$1/2$ pound finely diced pork belly

1 tablespoon soy sauce

2 teaspoons sugar

$1 1/2$ cups coarsely chopped sour kimchi with a bit of its liquid

1 container (14 ounces) firm tofu

Vegetable oil as necessary

Heat the sesame oil in a large nonstick skillet over high heat. Add the onion and garlic and cook just until fragrant, about 30 seconds. Add the pork belly and cook, stirring now and then, until the fat is rendered and the meat is browned, about 5 minutes. Add the soy sauce and sugar to the pork and stir to combine. Add the kimchi and its liquid, reduce the heat to medium, and cook until all of the flavors are combined, the pork is completely cooked through, and the vegetables are nicely softened, about 10 minutes.

Meanwhile, cut the tofu crosswise into $1/2$-inch-thick slices and steam or pan-fry them in a little vegetable oil in a nonstick pan just to get them warm. Mound the warm pork and kimchi mixture in the center of a serving platter and surround with the tofu slices. Eat by combining bites of tofu with the pork and kimchi mixture alongside cooked rice.

BEAN SPROUT SOUP

— SERVES 4 —

Simple, clean bean sprout soup is often eaten to ease hangovers. I read somewhere that the sprouts have lots of asparagines, an essential amino acid that works to lower acetaldehyde in the body, the chemical compound that is responsible for hangovers. I say eat up! This is my mother's recipe, quirks and all.

Rinse the bean sprouts under running water and set aside in a colander. Bring 6 cups of water to a boil in a large soup pot. Pack the anchovies into a metal strainer, add the strainer to the pot, and boil for 15 minutes. Remove the strainer and discard the anchovies. (Alternatively you can tie the anchovies in a piece of cheesecloth and fish it out of the stock.)

Add the sprouts, garlic, and *dashida* to the stock, cover, and boil for 5 minutes. My mother says it's important not to peek while the sprouts are boiling or else they will taste bitter. Serve the soup garnished with the scallions.

4 cups fresh mung bean or soybean sprouts

1 handful dried anchovies, heads and innards discarded

2 garlic cloves, finely minced

1 teaspoon dashida or fish sauce

2 scallions, thinly sliced

BUDAE JJIGAE (ARMY STEW)

— SERVES 4 TO 6 —

Budae jjigae translates to "army stew," a name that accurately describes the origin of this fascinating dish. It was developed with the ingredients that American GIs rationed to Koreans during the war, mid-century American stalwarts like Spam, hot dogs, and baked beans. By combining these decidedly non-Korean ingredients with staples like kimchi and *gochujang* (red pepper paste), Koreans were able to use what they were given to produce familiar flavors. The resulting stew, essentially a pork and cabbage stew with beans, is one of my absolute favorite dishes, something akin to a Korean cassoulet but spicier and cheesier. Since it's often eaten late at night after drinking, it's more of a hangover preventive rather than a cure. This is my Korean family's recipe, which includes not only American cheese but peanut butter too. I know it reads crazy, but it tastes unbelievable.

Bring the broth to a boil in a large soup pot. Add the onion, zucchini, kimchi, and Umma Paste. Cover and boil for 5 minutes. Add all of the meats, the cheese, pork and beans, and peanut butter. Return to a boil, cover, and cook for 10 minutes.

Add the ramen noodles (discard the seasoning packets) and cook just until the noodles are cooked, about 3 minutes. Top with scallions and serve to drunk friends to prevent terrible hangovers.

Note: I usually buy oxtail broth because it takes hours to make. (I get it from a restaurant in Manhattan's Koreatown on West 32nd Street, but it's also readily available at Korean grocery stores.) If you can't find or if you'd prefer to make it at home, simply cover oxtails with plenty of water, bring to a boil, and continue to cook at a rolling boil until the stock is cloudy and nearly white, about 6 hours. Be sure to check the water level as it's cooking to keep the bones covered. The cooked oxtails are a delicious cook's snack—try them with a little soy sauce and rice vinegar.

- 2 quarts oxtail broth (see Note)
- 1 yellow onion, chopped
- 2 zucchini, coarsely chopped
- 2 $1/2$ cups sour kimchi, rinsed and coarsely chopped
- Umma Paste (page 23)
- 2 hot dogs, sliced on the diagonal
- 8-inch piece of kielbasa, sliced on the diagonal
- 1 handful cocktail wieners, halved crosswise
- 1 can (12 ounces) Spam, diced
- $1/2$ slice American cheese
- One-third of a 14-ounce can pork and beans
- 1 teaspoon peanut butter
- 2 packages instant ramen noodles
- 3 scallions, thinly sliced

YUKGAEJANG (HANGOVER BEEF BRISKET SOUP)

— SERVES 4 TO 6 —

A spicy, hearty soup, *yukgaejang* will fortify you against anything, hangovers included. Note that Koreans like the chewy texture of boiled brisket, which is why this recipe only includes about 45 minutes of cooking time. For the American palate, you can cook the soup for up to $1\frac{1}{2}$ hours at a low simmer to make the meat more tender. Also note that if you can't find royal fern (a vegetable that has the texture of parsley stems and is a common ingredient in Korean royal court cuisine; it's available at most Korean markets), you can serve the soup over cooked noodles for added body and a similar texture, or substitute Japanese enoki mushrooms. You can make this with regular Umma Paste instead of Spicy Umma Paste if you don't have a huge tolerance for heat (that's you, Mr. Wolverine).

Heat the sesame oil in a large, heavy pot over high heat. Add the brisket and season with salt and pepper. Cook, stirring now and then, until browned on all sides, 3 to 4 minutes. Add the Spicy Umma Paste, leek, royal fern, onions, and beef broth. Add enough water just to cover the solids. Bring to a boil and skim off any foam that rises to the surface. Cover the pot and cook at a low boil until the meat is tender, about 40 minutes.

Add the bean sprouts and cook until they're tender, about 10 minutes. Serve hot with cooked rice and kimchi on the side.

2 tablespoons toasted sesame oil

$1\frac{1}{2}$ pounds lean beef brisket, thinly sliced

Coarse salt and freshly ground black pepper

$\frac{1}{4}$ cup Spicy Umma Paste (page 24)

1 large leek, cut into 2-inch pieces

1 package ($1\frac{1}{2}$ pounds) water-packed boiled royal fern, rinsed

2 medium yellow onions, coarsely chopped

4 cups beef broth (page 200)

4 cups mung bean sprouts

Cooked rice and kimchi, for serving

달콤한 한식

A LITTLE SOMETHING SWEET

In a country without many ovens, cakes and pastries and other typical Western desserts are nearly nonexistent. In Korea, a meal is generally finished with fresh fruit, usually melon or Korean pears. There is, however, big affection for confections. Candies and treats are often made with nuts and sweetened with honey; and sweet rice cakes, which come in a variety of colors and shapes, are hugely popular. The rice cakes, called *tteok* (pronounced "duck") look almost like French marzipan creations and are eaten both casually and during ritual meals like Chuseok, which is essentially Korean Thanksgiving. Koreans also love frozen desserts, and convenience stores have all sorts of amazing packaged ice creams, including sandwiches, bars, ice pops and more.

GREEN TEA GRANITA

— SERVES 6 TO 8 —

Inspired by the green tea we tasted on Jeju Island, this granita is one of my favorite things to serve after a Korean meal at home (desserts that you can make ahead of time are always great for a home cook!). If you can find green tea in powder form (a tip I learned from Jean-Georges), try it out—it's the quickest way to get a tremendous amount of green tea flavor and it imparts a more vibrant color than tea bags or leaves.

4 tablespoons green tea powder (see Note)

²⁄₃ cup honey

2 teaspoons finely grated fresh ginger

Grated zest of 1 lime

Fresh red currants (optional)

Whisk together the green tea powder, honey, ginger, and 4 cups cold water. Pour the granita mixture into a 9 x 13-inch baking pan or other shallow dish. Place the dish in the freezer and freeze until it's solid, at least 4 hours and up to 24.

Scrape the granita with a fork to make it flaky and serve in glasses or shallow bowls. (If you prefer you can scoop it when it's just frozen and more like a slushie.) Top each serving with a small grating of lime zest and a few red currants if you have them.

Note: If you can't find green tea powder, use 6 green tea bags. Bring 4 cups of water to a boil and pour over the tea bags in a large bowl and let it steep for 3 minutes. Discard the tea bags and whisk in the honey and ginger. Let the mixture cool before proceeding.

Green Tea

Aside from cocktails, green tea is probably the most prized beverage in Korea. When Susan Kim gave us a tour of the AmorePacific green tea fields on Jeju Island, we learned the ins and outs of green tea, including a close look at the plants themselves, the roasting process, and the variety of ways green tea is put to use. Perhaps the most important thing we learned was how to brew and consume green tea in the correct way. While the absolute best way to drink green tea is at the source, where it's grown and harvested, to make successful green tea at home, Susan advised us to use warm water (not boiling water, which induces bitterness) in order to give the tea a smooth taste. Add 5 grams (a generous teaspoon) for every cup of water. Steep the leaves for 1 minute, just enough time to soften them. After straining the tea into small cups, the traditional way to consume it is to balance the cup on your left hand, wrap your right hand around the cup, lift it up and observe the color, and then gently take a sip.

HOTTEOK (SWEET PANCAKES)

— MAKES 8 PANCAKES —

One of JG's favorite food finds from our trip was *hotteok*, which he ate during his visit to the Five Day Market on Jeju Island. These doughy, sweet pancakes are a popular street food all over Korea but are pretty easy to make at home. Just give yourself enough time to let the simple yeast dough rise and then stuff them with the traditional mixture of brown sugar and chopped nuts or with chocolate (JG's favorite)—yum!

PANCAKES

1 cup warm (110° to 120°F) water

1 envelope rapid-rise yeast (2¼ teaspoons)

2 tablespoons granulated sugar

Large pinch of coarse salt

1 tablespoon vegetable oil, plus more for cooking

2 cups flour, plus more for kneading the dough

FILLINGS (choose one)

½ cup packed dark brown sugar mixed with 3 tablespoons chopped peanuts, walnuts, or pine nuts

⅓ cup chopped dark chocolate

To make the dough: Stir together the water, yeast, salt, sugar, and 1 tablespoon oil in a large bow. Let it sit until the surface is cloudy and foamy, about 5 minutes. Stir in the flour. The dough will be quite sticky. Cover the bowl with a tea towel or plastic wrap and let it rise until doubled in size, at least 1 hour and up to 2.

Punch the dough down, cover, and let rise for 30 minutes.

Meanwhile, prepare whichever filling you're using and set aside.

To fry the pancakes: Generously flour a work surface and turn out the dough. Knead for just a minute, adding more flour if necessary, until the surface of the dough is nice and smooth. The dough will be quite shaggy, so don't be afraid to use lots of flour. Divide the dough into 8 equal pieces. Flatten each piece of dough with the palm of your hand. Divide the filling among the discs, mounding it in the center of each. Bring the dough together over the filling and seal each one so that no filling shows.

Heat a large nonstick skillet over medium heat and add a thin film of vegetable oil. Add 2 of the dough pieces and cook, seam-side down, until the underside is lightly browned, about 2 minutes. Turn each pancake and press down firmly with a spatula until it is about ½ inch thick. Cook until the second side is browned, about 2 minutes. Turn again onto the first side. Cover the pan and cook for 1 minute, just to ensure that the filling is melted. Blot the pancakes with paper towels and repeat until all of the pancakes are cooked. Serve while they're hot.

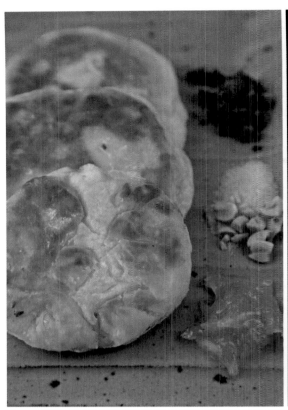

MAKGEOLLI ICE CREAM

SERVES 6

Makgeolli ice cream is a recipe inspired by a meal I ate at the Ninth Gate restaurant in Seoul. Dinner ended with a sorbet made with *makgeolli*, a very popular Korean alcoholic beverage brewed from rice. It was served in a little cup made of beet. Very cool (literally). On its own, *makgeolli* tastes like a sort of cross between sake and ale; transformed into a sorbet, it was a refreshing end to a rich meal. Turned into an ice cream sweetened with a bit of maple syrup, it becomes an unexpected, addictive dessert.

1$\frac{1}{2}$ **cups heavy cream**
1$\frac{1}{2}$ **cups makgeolli**
$\frac{1}{2}$ **cup maple syrup**
6 egg yolks
$\frac{1}{2}$ **cup sugar**
Chopped sesame seed brittle, for serving (recipe follows)
Raspberries, for serving
Maple syrup, for serving

Combine the heavy cream, *makgeolli,* and maple syrup in a medium saucepan. Bring to a simmer over medium-high heat.

Meanwhile, whisk the eggs yolks and sugar together in a large bowl.

Whisking constantly, slowly pour the hot cream mixture into the egg yolk mixture. Return the mixture to the saucepan and cook over low heat, stirring now and then, until thick enough to coat the back of a wooden spoon (swipe your finger across the wooden spoon and if the clean line holds its own, it's perfect), 4 to 5 minutes.

Pour the mixture through a fine sieve into a clean bowl and allow it to cool completely (you can speed this up by placing the bowl over a larger bowl of ice and water). Pour the ice cream mixture into an ice cream machine and freeze it according to the manufacturer's instructions.

Serve on its own or with chopped-up sesame brittle, raspberries, and a little drizzle of maple syrup.

SESAME SEED BRITTLE

— MAKES ABOUT 2 CUPS CHOPPED BRITTLE —

Using roasted sesame seeds boosts the nutty flavor of this crisp brittle, which is actually a breeze to make. It's not only the perfect topping for ice cream but also complements cocktails like the Ginger Georgie (page 212) wonderfully. Pack a few pieces in a lunchbox for a fun kids' treat.

Lightly oil a heavy rimmed baking sheet or use a silicon liner.

Stir together the sesame seeds, corn syrup, sugar, butter, and 2 tablespoons of water in a large, heavy saucepan. Bring to a boil over high heat, lower the heat to medium and cook, stirring now and then, until dark golden brown, 15 minutes (or until the temperature reaches 270°F when measured with a candy thermometer).

Take the mixture off the heat and stir in the baking soda and then turn out onto the prepared baking sheet. Use a spoon to spread the mixture evenly to a ½-inch thickness. Let the brittle cool completely, then roughly chop or break into pieces with your hands.

Canola oil, for the pan
1 cup roasted sesame seeds
½ cup light corn syrup
½ cup sugar
1 tablespoon unsalted butter
½ teaspoon baking soda

Acknowledgments

would like to thank the people who made this book happen!

First I would like to thank Julia Turshen, my coauthor, for her enthusiasm, knowledge, and overall wonderfulness.

Thank you to Charlie Pinsky and Eric Rhee from Frappé Inc. for making this project a reality and letting me be a part of this amazing journey. And to Don, Sam, Brandon, Gary, HyunJun, BK, Jae, and Juan and his team at GRS. Thank you also to Jennifer, Cathy, and especially Diana. Thanks go to the Jackman family and Heather Graham.

Thank you to Andre Baranowski for his evocative food photography and to April Lee for her amazing food styling. Her smile and calm got us through many a stressful day! And to Mrs. Rhee. And thank you to Seyoung Oh and Tom Caltabiano, our talented location photographers. And also to Jiyeon Lee for her help.

Thank you to Rodale for believing in me, a home cook, and letting me do this my way.

I would like to thank my amazing husband, Jean-Georges, for his love and support. Thank you for encouraging me to "keep it simple." Easy for him to say! But he is always right.

I would like to thank my daughter, Chloe, for being the light of my life. I know that you were meant to be mine. I am so proud to be your mother and I love you so very much. Your love of Korean cuisine made me do my research and push myself to try new things.

Thank you to all the Vongerichten family, here and abroad, for embracing my culture and me. Thank you for being my taste testers.

Thank you to my sister, Kai, and my brother, Rick, for loving me and giving me immeasurable support.

To my mother Suki, the one who gave me life. Thank you for loving me and being there for the second act of my life and for always believing I can do anything.

To my mother Margo, the one who taught me how to live my life. Thank you for loving me and taking care of me, not just physically but emotionally. You were the one who was there for me—every Band-Aid, every test, every milestone in my life, and you did it with such love and support. It's because of you that I am the woman I am today. Thank you for encouraging my cooking from such a young age. Thank you for eating my dry scrambled eggs and burned muffins and remaining enthusiastic about me trying a new recipe for dinner. You are my rock!

To my father, Colonel James P. Allen Jr. Thank you for loving me and supporting me. You were always the real cook in the family and you sure set the bar high. I still can't get that cheesecake recipe right!

—Marja

Major, major thanks to Team Frappé (especially to Charlie, the giver of great opportunities), to the Vongerichten family (whose generosity is unparalleled), and to Pam Krauss and Kara Plikaitis.

—Julia

감사드릴 분들

And for their support,
thank you to:

First Lady of the Republic of Korea

Office of the President, the Republic of Korea

Visit Korea Committee

Korean Food Foundation

Ministry for Food, Agriculture, Forestry and Fisheries

Ministry of Culture, Sports and Tourism

Hite Jinro Group

CJ CheilJedang

CJ Foodville

Samsung

AMOREPACIFIC

H Mart

Westin Chosun Hotels

Korean Air

Yido Pottery

Le Creuset

All-Clad

Cuisinart

John Boos

RESOURCES

for Korean Ingredients and Equipment

Most of the ingredients called for in this book are available at your local Korean or Asian grocery store. If not, check out these great online sources.

www.aeriskitchen.com is a great reference for Korean recipes.

www.amazon.com seems to have just about everything a Korean cook might need, including Korean cookbooks, music, and a great selection of ingredients from their grocery section.

www.hmart.com is a great Korean grocery store with locations that include those I visit nearly every week in New York and New Jersey. Their website is very helpful for finding great ingredients.

www.kgrocer.com is my go-to source for ordering Korean ingredients online. They stock everything!

www.maangchi.com is perhaps the most informative Korean cooking blog around. The website started as a video series and has expanded into a great reference tool that includes not only videos, but also recipes and descriptions of ingredients. I reference it often.

www.seouleats.com and **www.fatmanseoul.com** are terrific Korea-based food blogs written in English, especially helpful if you're planning a trip and want good restaurant tips.

Photo Credits

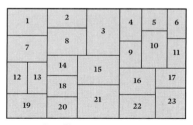

Pages xxii–xxiii

Photos: 4, 17 by Andre Baranowski;
7, 8, 10, 11, 12, 16, 18, 19, 20, 21, 22 by
Seyoung Oh; 1, 2, 3, 5, 6, 9, 13, 14, 15, 23
by Tom Caltabiano; 5 by Pil Oh

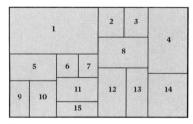

Pages 2–3

Photos: 1 by Seyoung Oh; all others by Andre
Baranowski

Tom Caltabiano:
pages x–xi, 22, 26, 89, 114–115, 133, 137, 144, 146–147, 202, 204–205

Pil Oh:
pages 5, 20–21, 30–35, 52, 118–119

Seyoung Oh:
pages xix, xxi, 15, 55, 68, 76, 99, 103, 114–115, 125, 132, 146, 152–153, 158–160, 163, 166–167, 169, 174–175, 179, 196, 198, 226–227, 233, 236–237

Index

Underscored page references indicate boxed text. **Boldfaced** page references indicate photographs.